WOMEN OF COLOR
IN THE UNITED STATES

GARLAND REFERENCE LIBRARY
OF SOCIAL SCIENCE
(VOL. 469)

WOMEN OF COLOR
IN THE UNITED STATES
A Guide to the Literature

Bernice Redfern

GARLAND PUBLISHING, INC. • NEW YORK & LONDON
1989

Library of Congress Cataloging-in-Publication Data

Redfern, Bernice, 1947–.
    Women of color in the United States : a guide to the literature /
Bernice Redfern.
        p.   cm. — (Garland reference library of social science; v.
469)
    Includes index.
    ISBN 0–8240–5849–6 (alk. paper)
    1. Minority women—United States—Bibliography.   2. Afro-American
women—Bibliography.   I. Title.   II. Series.
Z7964.U49R4   1989
[HQ1410]   88-24614 √
                                                                CIP

Printed on acid-free, 250-year-life paper
Manufactured in the United States of America

CONTENTS

PREFACE

In the last ten to fifteen years there has been a tremendous increase in the volume of literature by and about Afro-American women in the United States. There are several good bibliographies which provide access to the literature on black women from the nineteenth century through the late 1970s. For this reason, I have decided to focus on the recent literature. With a few exceptions, I have not included anything published before 1975. The primary purpose of this bibliography is to list scholarly books, journal articles, significant chapters in books, and dissertations. I have excluded all but the most significant popular books and periodical literature. Fiction and poetry, except in mixed form anthologies, has also been excluded. I have not attempted to list works dealing with the family unless they pertain specifically to the role of women in the family. Medical literature and materials dealing with health issues such as abortion have been excluded.

Individual essays of a scholarly nature contained in general anthologies have been listed separately and references to the collective work have been inserted.

Chapters two, three, and four contain works about Asian American, Hispanic American, and Native American women. The literature on these groups is less extensive than the literature on black women, so these chapters are considerably shorter than the first chapter.

Because of the difficulty involved in obtaining dissertations, annotations for dissertations listed in this bibliography have been summarized from *Dissertations Abstracts International.*

Each chapter begins with a brief overview of the literature. Chapters are organized by subcategories as dictated by the content of the material. Within each subcategory items are listed alphabetically. The reader should keep in mind that since much of the material is interdisciplinary in nature, some items could have been placed in more than one subcategory. I selected categories which seemed most appropriate. Cross-references have been inserted to direct the reader to these items, and subject and author indexes are provided to facilitate use.

Women of Color
In the United States

CHAPTER 1

AFRO-AMERICAN WOMEN

This chapter contains literature about Afro-American women. A majority of it is written by black women. Throughout this section I have interchanged use of the terms black, Afro-American, and women of color.

An area where Afro-American women have made a significant contribution is the field of education. Black women have opened schools and been leaders in education since before the Civil War. They have overcome great odds to become school administrators, although as the publications in this subsection suggest, they are still underrepresented in academic institutions and at the administrative level.

A large part of the current literature is concerned with the ramifications of racial and gender discrimination on employment of black women.

Another large section is focused on the complex issues of sexism in the black liberation movement and racism in the women's movement. Publications concerned with these issues are included in the subsection on feminism and women's studies. Also grouped under this heading are works dealing with black feminism, black women's studies, black women in black studies, and black lesbianism.

The subsection on history and politics lists articles and books describing the leadership role taken by black women in various social movements such as the abolitionist movement and the women's club movement among others.

A great deal of the current material about black women is concerned with Afro-American women as writers and artists reflecting the current renaissance in black women's literature. In this subsection I have placed works on music, fine arts, and literature.

The subsection on social science contains a mixed group of materials in the disciplines of psychology, sociology, social work, and anthropology. Some of the subjects treated here are sex role attitudes, self-esteem, fear of success, and coping strategies used to deal with poverty and discrimination.

Bibliographies

1. Davis, Lenwood G. *The Black Woman in American Society: A Selected Annotated Bibliography.* Boston: G.K. Hall, 1975.

   Covers all periods of history from earliest times to the present. Contains references to books, periodical articles, reference works, reports, pamphlets, speeches and government publications. Particularly strong on auto-biographies. Also contains a listing of the major black history collections.

2. Klotman, Phyllis R., and Wilmer H. Baatz, comps. *The Black Family and the Black Woman: A Bibliography.* New York: Arno Press, 1978.

   A partially annotated bibliography containing popular and scholarly works. Includes a wide variety of materials: books, periodical articles, ERIC documents, children's books, speeches and audiovisual materials.

3. Richardson, Marilyn. *Black Women and Religion: A Bibliography.* Boston: G.K. Hall, 1980.

   An annotated bibliography covering literature (including fiction, drama, and poetry), music, art and audiovisual materials.

4. Roberts, J.C., comp. *Black Lesbians: An Annotated Bibliography.* Weatherby Lake, Missouri: Naiad Press, 1981.

   An annotated guide to materials by and/or about black lesbians in the United States. Lists poetry, fiction, book reviews, recordings, filmed interviews, books, periodical articles, position papers, and unpublished material

5. Sims, Janet. "The Afro-American Woman: Researching Her History." *Reference Service Review* 11, no.1 (Spring 1980): 9-30.

   An annotated bibliography listing autobiographies, biographies, life histories, dissertations and masters' theses by and about black women. Organized alphabetically by last name. Includes popular as well as scholarly works.

6. Sims, Janet. *The Progress of Afro-American Women: A Selected Bibliography and Resource Guide.* Westport, Conn.: Greenwood Press, 1980.

   An unannotated bibliography which includes nineteenth and twentieth-century materials on Afro-American women. Includes both popular and scholarly works. Contains a section on slave narratives and a separate section on special periodical issues devoted to black women.

7. Stevenson, Rosemary M. "Black Women in the United States: A Bibliographical Essay." *Sage Race Relations Abstracts* 8, no.4 (November 1983): 1-19.

   Emphasizes literature published since 1970 which focuses on current conditions and struggles.

8. Stevenson, Rosemary M. "Black Women in the United States: A Bibliography of Recent Works." *The Black Scholar* 16, no.2 (March/April 1985): 45- 49.

   This short, unannotated list focuses on publications since 1975. It has sections on biography, autobiography, history, literature, economic issues, social conditions, psychological and mental health, feminism and women's studies.

9. Stone, Pauline T. *The Black American Woman in the Social Science Literature.* Ann Arbor, Mich.: Women's Studies Program, University of Michigan, 1978.

   Brings together materials written on the interaction between racism and sexism in American society up until the middle of 1978. Includes references to unpublished papers, speeches, newspaper items, dissertations and theses, ERIC documents, as well as published books and articles. Does not contain annotations.

10. Washington, Sarah M. "An Annotated Bibliography of Black Women Biographies and Autobiographies for Secondary School Students." Ph.D. diss., University of Illinois, Urbana-Champaign, 1980.

    Lists sixty-eight biographies and autobiographies arranged according to the careers of the women who are surveyed here. Suggestions for reading level appeal are given.

11. Williams, Ora. *American Black Women in the Arts and Social Sciences: A Bibliography.* Revised Edition. Metuchen, N.J.: Scarecrow Press, 1978.

    The primary purpose of this unannotated bibliography is to highlight the achievements of black women authors. With some exceptions, the references are to works by American black women. Contains scholarly and popular books, journal and magazine articles, plays, poetry, novels, juvenile literature, audiovisual materials, music and musical recordings. A chronology of significant dates and accomplishments of black women is also included.

General Works

12.   Harley, Sharon, and Rosalyn Terborg-Penn, eds. *The Afro-American Woman: Struggles and Images.* Port Washington, N.Y.: Kennikat Press, 1978.

A collection of scholarly papers on a wide range of topics including history, literature, music, education, and politics. Contains items 37, 53, 114, 208, 222, 267, and 316.

13.   Hawks, Joanne V., and Sheila L. Skemp, eds. *Sex, Race, and the Role of Women in the South.* Jackson, Miss.: University Press of Mississippi, 1983.

Contains papers presented at a symposium on southern history. All of the papers in this collection point out that race divided southern women, retarding a strong women's movement in this region. Contains item 113.

14.   Martin, Elmer P., and Joanne M. Martin. "The Black Woman: Perspectives on Her Role in the Family." in *Ethnicity and Women.* Edited by Winston A. Van Horne and Thomas V. Tonnesen. University of Wisconsin System, American Ethnic Studies Coordinating Committee, 1986, pp. 184-204.

Authors decry the negative image of black women seen in public opinion, the media, and the social sciences. They believe destructive stereotypes of black women as matriarchs and "welfare bums" must be replaced with more positive images which depict black women as hard-working, achieving people seeking to improve the quality of their lives.

15.   Murray, Saundra R., and Daphne D. Harrison. "Black Women and the Future." *Psychology of Women Quarterly* 6, no.1 (Fall 1981): 113-122.

Focuses on the future role of black women. Discusses marital status, labor force participation, and black women as religious and community leaders. Sees travel to Africa and marriage to African men as important options for American black women in the future.

16.   Rodgers-Rose, La Frances, ed. *The Black Woman.* Beverly Hills, Calif.: Sage Publications, 1980.

This is a collection of interviews, original research, and theory papers by black women about black women. Includes articles by sixteen women covering all phases of the lives of Afro-American women: family life, demographic characteristics, social psychology of the black woman, relationships between men and women, and political, educational and economic institutions.   Contains items 105, 128, and 161.

17.   Steady, Filomina C. ed. *The Black Woman Cross-Culturally*. Cambridge, Mass.: Schenkman Publishing Co., 1981.

Part II of this collection contains articles on black women in the United States on a variety of topics including literature and music, myth of the black matriarchy, black women in the nineteenth-century women's movement, and black women prisoners in present day South Carolina. Contains items 213, 225, and 232.

18.   Swerdlow, Amy, and Hanna Lessinger, eds. *Class, Race, and Sex: The Dynamics of Control*. Boston: G.K. Hall, 1983.

A collection of essays on diverse topics, some of which are black women and work, feminist theology and black women, the women's liberation movement and black women, life styles of black families, and welfare and racism. Contains items 117 and 156.

19.   Washington, Patricia L. "The Black Woman's Agenda: An Investigation into Strategies for Change." Ph.D. diss., Arizona State University, 1978.

Uses content analysis of discussions held at the "Black Woman and the Bicentennial" conference. Discussions concerned strategies for affecting change in broad areas such as employment and education. Action oriented words were used to identify the strategies. Results of the study were used to make recommendations for further research.

20.   Webber, Kikanza N. "Reflections on Black American Women: The Images of the Eighties." *Western Journal of Black Studies* 4, no.4 (Winter 1980): 242-250.

Discusses five stereotyped images of black women that can be found in scholarly and popular literature: the Noble Slave, the Manipulating Matriarch, Sweet Meat Mama, the Revolutionary Sister, and the Women's Lib Lackey. The author asserts that black women and men should work together to fight racism which is a more important struggle than the fight against sexism.

Autobiography, Biography, Life Histories

21.   Aba-Mecha, Barbara W. "Black Woman Activist in Twentieth Century South Carolina: Modjeska Monteith Simkins." Ph.D. diss., Emory University, 1978.

A biographical study of a civil rights activist in South Carolina. Discusses her work with local, state, regional, and national organizations during the 1940s and the 1950s.

22. Alexander, Estelle C. "Tell Them So You'll Know." Ph.D. diss., University of Iowa, 1984.

A two volume work which studies the art of autobiography. Alexander studied the autobiographies of Maya Angelou, Zora Neale Hurston, Nikki Giovanni, and Gwendolyn Brooks as preparation for writing her own autobiography which is contained in the first volume. Volume two is a commentary on the process of composing autobiography.

23. Angelou, Maya. *All God's Children Need Traveling Shoes*. New York: Random House, 1986.

Ms. Angelou continues her autobiography with an account of her sojourn in Africa. Her marriage to a South African freedom fighter has ended, and she has traveled to Ghana to enroll her son in college. When he is seriously injured in an automobile accident, she is forced to change her plans and remain in Ghana. She takes a job as an administrative assistant at the University of Ghana in order to pay her son's tuition.

24. Angelou, Maya. *The Heart of a Woman*. New York: Random House, 1981.

In the fourth book of her autobiography Ms. Angelou moves to New York and joins the Harlem Writers Guild in order to begin her career as a writer. She becomes active in the Southern Christian Leadership Conference, and meets Martin Luther King and Malcom X. While engaged to another man, she meets and falls in love with a South African freedom fighter. She marries him and moves to Africa.

25. Angelou, Maya. *Singin' and Swingin' and Gettin' Merry Like Christmas*. New York: Random House, 1976.

The third volume of Ms. Angelou's continuing autobiography. She tells of her struggle to support herself and her son, her brief marriage to a white man, her entrance into show business, and her experiences in Europe and Africa while touring in "Porgy and Bess."

26. Blackburn, Regina L. "Conscious Agents of Time and Self: The Lives and Styles of African-American Women as Seen Through Their Autobiographical Writings." Ph.D. diss., University of New Mexico, 1978.

Studies autobiographies of black women to discover what is revealed about their lives, self-concepts, and development. Covers the period of slavery until the present. Includes chapters on sex, love, and marriage; search for the black female self, work, childhood and related experiences.

27. Braxton, Joanne M. "Autobiography By Black Women: A Tradition Within a Tradition." Ph.D. diss., Yale University, 1984.

Examines a number of autobiographies of black women from the nineteenth century to the present including those of Charlotte L. Forten, Susie King Taylor, Ida B. Wells, Zora Neale Hurston, and Maya Angelou. The purpose of this study is to identify autobiography of American black women as a tradition.

28. Brooks, Sara. *You May Plow Here: The Narrative of Sara Brooks*. Edited and Photographed by Thordis Simonsen. New York: Simon and Schuster, 1987.

Sara Brooks tells of her childhood on an Alabama farm. Her speech has been rendered verbatim to preserve the distinctiveness of her voice. An insightful, inspiring account of black rural life in the early years of the twentieth century.

29. Buss, Fran L., comp. *Dignity: Lower Income Women Tell of Their Lives and Struggles*. Ann Arbor, Mich.: University of Michigan Press, 1985.

A collection of life stories of ten lower-income women. They come from a variety of racial/ethnic groups including one Native American, one of Japanese ancestry, a Mexican-American woman, three black women, and four white women. All of these women are survivors who have struggled to overcome poverty. All three black women grew up in the South and speak of their experiences with racial prejudice as well as poverty. Contains items 391, 452 and 568.

30. Calderon, Erma. *Erma: A Black Woman Remembers: 1912-1980*. New York: Random House, 1981.

An autobiography of a southern black woman as told to Leonard Ray Tell. Orphaned at the age of nine, Erma ran away from home to Florida where she worked in a store. She married at the age of eleven and gave birth to her first child at the age of twelve. She speaks of her experiences living in New York during the Depression.

31. Cazort, Jean. *Born to Play: The Life and Career of Hazel Harrison*. Westport, Conn.: Greenwood Press, 1983.

A biography of the concert pianist, Hazel Harrison (1883-1969).
It is based on archival sources and interviews with friends and
relatives of Ms. Harrison.

32. Cooke, Paul P. "Anna J. Cooper: Educator and Humanitarian."
     Negro History Bulletin 45 (January-March 1982): 5-7.

     Outlines the career of this highly educated woman. Born in
     slavery, she received bachelor's and master's degrees from
     Oberlin and she completed her Ph.D. in 1925 at the Sorbonne.
     She was a teacher, high school principal, college president, and
     was active in the women's club movement.

33. Crowder, Ralph L. "Black Women: A Neglected Dimension in
     History." *Black Collegian* 9 (May-June 1979): 103-109.

     Discusses six women whom the author believes are representative
     of the active role taken by black women in American life.
     These women are: Ida B. Wells, journalist and leader of the
     anti-lynching crusade; Lucy Gathering Parsons, labor activist and
     founding member of the Industrial Workers of the World; Sarah
     Evans Lewis, founder of a pioneer farming settlement; Mattie
     Proctor Thompson, cosmetologist, community leader, and model
     of black self-reliance; and Esland Goode Robeson, wife of Paul
     Robeson and author in her own right.

34. Davis, Marianna W., ed. *Contributions of Black Women to America.*
     Columbia, South Carolina: Kenday Press, 1982.

     A collection of short biographies of black women who have made
     significant contributions to American life. Volume I contains
     sketches of black women in the arts, media, business, law, and
     sports. Volume II contains women in civil rights, education,
     medicine and health, politics and government, and science.
     Research for this work was based as much as possible on
     primary sources including interviews, family papers, and church
     records.

35. Dunbar-Nelson, Alice M. *Give Us Each Day: The Diary of Alice
     Dunbar-Nelson.* Edited by Gloria T. Hull. New York: Norton,
     1984.

     This is the edited version of six manuscript diaries covering the
     period 1921 to 1931. Alice Dunbar-Nelson was a highly regarded
     poet before she married Paul Laurence Dunbar. Besides writing,
     she was also active in the National Federation of Colored
     Women's Clubs, the women's suffrage movement, and the crusade
     to end lynching. She was a platform speaker and, together with
     her second husband, Robert J. Nelson, published a progressive
     black newspaper. Her diary reveals a multi-faceted personality

who pursued many diverse interests and causes with great
energy. At the same time, she suffered the consequences of
living in a sexist society in that she was overshadowed by the
memory of her famous first husband.

36.   Fleming, John E. "Slavery, Civil War and Reconstruction: A Study
      of Black Women in Microcosm." *Negro History Bulletin* 38, no.6
      (1975): 430-433.

      Brief biographies of three black women, all former slaves, who
      worked to help the newly emancipated slaves: Sojourner Truth,
      Susie King Taylor, and Octavia Rogers Albert. Mrs. Albert
      collected and published a series of slave narratives. Susie King
      Taylor was a nurse, laundress, and teacher during the Civil War.
      She later published her memoirs of her experiences during the
      war.

*   Govan, Sandra Y. "Gwendolyn Bennett: Portrait of an Artist Lost."
      Cited below as item 259.

37.   Harley, Sharon. "Anna J. Cooper: A Voice for Black Women." in
      The Afro-American Woman: Struggles and Images. Edited by
      Sharon Harley and Rosalyn Terborg-Penn. Port Washington,
      N.Y.: Kennikat Press, 1978, pp. 87-96.

      Discusses the work of this noted black woman educator in the
      areas of Pan-Africanism, women's rights, education for black
      youth (particularly young black women), and racial equality.

*   Hemenway, Robert E. *Zora Neale Hurston: A Literary Biography.*
      Cited below as item 268.

*   Howard, Lillie P. *Zora Neale Hurston.* Cited below as item 273.

*   Hurston, Zora Neale. *Dust Tracks on a Road: An Autobiography.*
      2nd ed. Cited below as item 278.

38.   Hutton, Mary M.B. "The Rhetoric of Ida B. Wells: The Genesis of
      the Anti-Lynching Movement." Ph.D. diss., Indiana University,
      1975.

      An in-depth study of Ida B. Wells and her part in the anti-
      lynching movement. Outlines the rhetorical strategies she used
      to further her goals.

39.   Jones, Bessie. *For the Ancestors: Autobiographical Memories.*
      Urbana, Ill.: University of Illinois Press, 1983.

      The life story of an eighty year old singer of black spirituals
      whose life was dedicated to preserving traditional slave songs.
      As a member of the Georgia Sea Island Singers she performed

throughout the United States. Her story is recorded here by John Stewart, an anthropologist at the University of Illinois.

40. Jordan, Barbara, and Shelby Hearon. *Barbara Jordan: A Self-Portrait.* New York: Doubleday, 1979.

In this autobiography Barbara Jordan recalls her childhood growing up in Houston's Fourth Ward, a segregated neighborhood. She tells of her struggle to succeed at Boston University Law School and her entrance into Texas politics. She discusses her career as a Congresswoman and her role in the impeachment proceedings against President Nixon.

*   Lieb, Sandra R. *Mother of the Blues: A Study of Ma Rainey.* Cited below as item 289.

41. Lorde, Audre. *Zami: A New Spelling of My Name.* Trumansburg, New York: The Crossing Press, 1982.

This is the autobiography of the poet and black lesbian feminist, Audre Lorde. The daughter of Grenadian immigrants, she grew up in Harlem. She recounts her experiences with racism, especially while attending an all white high school. Lorde writes of the quiet strength and dignity of her mother. She tells of her growing awareness of her attraction for women and her first affair with a female coworker. She talks of her isolation in the 1950s when black women could not openly admit they were lesbians.

42. Lyons, Sylvia R. "Afro-American Women: The Outstanding and the Obscure." *Quarterly Journal of the Library of Congress* 32, no.4 (October 1975): 307-321.

Biographical profiles of three Afro-American women: Anna Murray Douglass (wife of Frederick Douglass), Mary Church Terrell, and Ruth Anna Fisher. The latter was an archivist employed by the Library of Congress. This article is based on primary sources housed in the Manuscript Division of the Library of Congress.

43. McFarlin, Annjennette S. "Hallie Quinn Brown: Black Woman Elocutionist." *Southern Speech Communication Journal* 46 (Fall 1980): 72-82.

Investigates the life of this little-known woman who was an educator and activist in social and political causes such as the anti-lynching crusade. She was a professor of elocution and public speaking at Wilberforce University. In 1920 she was elected president of the National Association of Colored Women, an office which she held for two terms. Sources used for this article include Brown's diary and her autobiography, *As the Mantle Falls*, which was never published.

* Moutoussamy-Ashe, Jeanne. *Viewfinders: Black Women Photographers, 1839-1985.* Cited below as item 301.

44. Murray, Pauli. *Song in a Weary Throat: An American Pilgrimage.* New York: Harper and Row, 1987.

   The autobiography of a civil rights activist, lawyer, writer, professor, feminist, and a founding member of The National Organization for Women. She tells of her determination to attend a non-segregated college and her struggle to gain admittance to Hunter College. She was one of four black women to graduate from Hunter in 1933. She writes of her deepening involvement in desegregation and civil rights causes in the 1930s and 1940s and of her growing friendship with Eleanor Roosevelt. Her interest in feminism was aroused when she attended Howard University Law School and was the only woman in her class. She describes her efforts in gaining passage of Title VII of the Civil Rights Act of 1964 with the stipulation that sex as well as race be included. This account ends before her ordination as an Episcopal priest.

* Shaw, Harry B. *Gwendolyn Brooks.* Cited below as item 320.

45. Sterling, Dorothy. *Black Foremothers: Three Lives.* Old Westbury, New York: The Feminist Press, 1979.

   Contains the biographies of three women: Ellen Craft, Ida B. Wells, and Mary Church Terrell. Ellen Craft escaped from slavery disguised as a young white gentleman along with her husband, William, who posed as her servant. She was later active in the abolitionist cause and was a teacher among the freed slaves. A chronology of each woman's life is included. Written in clear straightforward prose.

* See also item 229.

46. Thompson, Mildred. "Ida B. Wells-Barnett: An Exploratory Study of an American Black Woman, 1893-1930." Ph.D. diss., George Washington University, 1979.

   A biographical study of the famed journalist and anti-lynching crusader. Thompson says that although Wells was successful in her efforts to convert public sentiment and pass state laws against lynching, her later activities gained her little recognition from race leaders.

47.   White, Gloria M. "Mary Church Terrell: Organizer of Black
       Women." *Integrated Education* 17, (September-December 1980):
       2-8.

       Describes Mrs. Terrell's contributions to the education of blacks
       and her leadership in such organizations as the National
       Association for the Advancement of Colored People and The
       National Association of Colored Women.

48.   Williams, Ora. "An In-Depth Portrait of Alice Dunbar-Nelson."
       Ph.D. diss., University of California at Irvine, 1974.

       Seeks to validate Alice Dunbar-Nelson as a writer and
       personality and rescue her from obscurity. Maintains she was a
       true Renaissance woman who excelled at the many activities she
       involved herself in such as teaching, lecturing, editing, political
       and social service activities. Says that her invisibility is due to
       racism, sexism and her own literary integrity.

49.   Wilson, Emily H. *Hope and Dignity: Older Black Women of the
       South*. Philadelphia: Temple University Press, 1983.

       A collection of oral histories of older black women. The author
       traveled throughout North Carolina interviewing women over the
       age of sixty-five who had lived most of their lives in the South.
       Wilson is white which accounts for the fact that some of the
       women are less open than others about their experiences and
       views concerning racial discrimination.

Education

50.   Arnez, Nancy L. "Selected Black Female Superintendents of Public
       School Systems." *Journal of Negro Education* 51, no.3 (Summer
       1982): 309-317.

       Focuses on the achievements of two contemporary black women
       school administrators: Barbara A. Sizemore, former School
       Superintendent of the District of Columbia Public School System;
       and Ruth B. Love, General Superintendent of the Chicago Public
       School System.

51.   Artis-Goodwin, Sharon E. "Professional Barriers and Facilitators
       for Minority Women in Education Research." Ed.D. diss.,
       Harvard University, 1986.

       The purpose of this study is to identify barriers to career
       development of minority women which includes black,
       Asian/Pacific, American Indian, and Hispanic women as
       participants in the sample. Three major barriers are iden-

tified: lack of access to information, sexism, and limited funds for study and research.

52. Ashburn, Elizabeth A. "Influences and Motivations for Black and White Women to Attain Positions in a Male Dominated Profession." Ph.D. diss., State University of New York at Buffalo, 1979.

Surveyed twenty-eight black and thirty-two white women Ph.D's employed full-time in university positions. Concluded that black women perceived education as a means to career advancement and financial security.

53. Barnett, Evelyn B. "Nannie Burroughs and the Education of Black Women." in *The Afro-American Woman: Struggles and Images*. Edited by Sharon Harley and Rosalyn Terborg-Penn. Port Washington, N.Y.: Kennikat Press, 1978.

Describes the efforts of this little-known black educator to establish a vocational school for black girls. Burroughs also fought for women's suffrage and racial equality, and she promoted the study of Afro-American history and culture.

54. Bell-Scott, Patricia. "Black Women's Higher Education: Our Legacy." *Sage: A Scholarly Journal on Black Women* 1, no.1 (Spring 1984): 8-11.

Outlines the history of higher education for black women with special attention to Spelman and Bennett Colleges. Discusses some of the issues and questions that emerged with the development of separate institutions of higher education for black women.

55. Bell-Scott, Patricia. "Schoolin' 'Respectable' Ladies of Color: Issues in the History of Black Women's Higher Education." *Journal of the National Association for Women Deans, Administrators and Counselors* 43 (Winter 1979): 22-28.

See item 54.

56. Berry, Mary F. "Twentieth Century Black Women In Education." *Journal of Negro Education* 51, no.3 (Summer 1982): 288-300.

Emphasizes the contributions of five twentieth-century black women to education: Mary McLeod Bethune, Barbara Sizemore, Constance Baker Motley, Willa Beatrice Player, and Marian Wright Edelman. Also briefly discusses several other Afro-American women who have made contributions to further the educational goals of black people in the past twenty years.

57. Blackwell, Barbara G. "The Advocacies and Ideological
     Commitments of a Black Educator: Mary McCleod Bethune
     1875-1955." Ph.D. diss., The University of Connecticut, 1979.

     Focuses on this well-known educator's cultural roots; her
     philosophy of education; her involvement in civic, religious, and
     social clubs for black women and the influence of them on
     educational reform.

58. Clier-Thomas, Bettye. "The Impact of Black women In Education: An
     Historical Overview." *Journal of Negro Education* 51, no.3
     (Summer 1982): 173-180.

     An introductory article to a special issue devoted to black
     women in education. Provides a brief overview of the history
     of black women in education.

59. Cotton, Julia V. "Role Perceptions and Characteristics of Black
     Female Administrators in institutions of Higher Education in
     Tennessee." Ph.D. diss., University of Pittsburgh, 1979.

     Surveyed 142 black female administrators, examining such factors
     as salaries, academic rank, tenure status, and highest degree
     held.

60. Ellis, Mary H. "Upward Mobility Patterns of Black and White
     Women in Higher Education Administration." Ed.D. diss., The
     University of Alabama, 1982.

     Used interviews to gather data for case studies of twenty-one
     black and twenty-five white women administrators who have
     reached the level of dean in a four year college or university.
     Found more similarities than differences between the two groups
     of women. Sexism and racism had been experienced by all of
     the women in the study, with racism a greater problem for black
     women.

61. Fleming, Jacqueline. "Black Women in Black and White College
     Environments: The Making of a Matriarch." *Journal of Social
     Issues* 39, no.3 (Fall 1983): 41-54.

     Compares the impact of attending a black college as opposed to
     attending a predominantly white college for black women.
     Tested a sample of over five hundred black female freshman or
     senior students at one of four predominantly white colleges or
     in one of two all black colleges. Preliminary results indicate
     that adverse conditions at predominantly white colleges
     contributed to personal characteristics such as self-assertiveness
     which are closely bound to the black matriarch stereotype.
     Women who attended the all black colleges made greater

academic gains and experienced more social support, but this appeared to contribute to social passivity, reflecting the image of black women as victims of double jeopardy.

62. Graber, Anita W. "Imagining the World: the Reflections and Perceptions of Black Low-Income Mothers in Relation to Their Involvements in the Educational Lives of Their Children." Ed.D. diss., Columbia University Teachers College, 1982.

Investigated the involvement of black, low-income mothers in their children's education. The author was especially interested in how this involvement was seen by school personnel. Based on taped interviews with twenty-two mothers and fourteen school staff members. All the mothers shared a common belief in the value of education.

63. Grant, Linda. "Black Females 'Place' in Desegregated Classrooms." *Sociology of Education* 57 (April 1984): 98-110.

Grant observed the experiences of black female students in six desegregated first grade classes. Five of the six teachers were interviewed in-depth about the black female students in their classrooms. Teachers' evaluations, teachers' behaviors toward students, students' orientations toward teachers, and peer interactions were examined. Findings indicate that black girls received less praise for their academic skills than did white girls. Teachers emphasized black girls' social skills rather than their academic skills. Grant contends that their schooling experiences may push black girls to assume stereotyped female roles rather than to strive for achievement.

64. Guy-Sheftall, Beverly. "Black Women and Higher Education: Spelman and Bennett Colleges Revisited." *Journal of Negro Education* 51, no.3 (Summer 1982): 278-287.

Discusses the impact black women's colleges (specifically Spelman and Bennett Colleges) have had on educational opportunities for black women.

65. Hamilton, Kelly. *Goals and Plans of Black Women: A Sociological Study*. Hicksville, New York: Exposition Press, 1975.

Examined the effects of attending a predominantly black or racially integrated university on the level of achievement of black females. Results indicate that the subjects' educational plans tended to be influenced more by their socio-economic class than the type of school they attended.

66. Harley, Sharon. "Beyond the Classroom: The Organizational Lives of Black Female Educators In the District of Columbia,

1890-1930." *Journal of Negro Education* 51, no.3 (Summer 1982): 254-265.

Explores the organized charitable activities of black female educators in Washington D.C. at the turn of the twentieth century.

67. Henle, Ellen, and Marlene Merrill. "Antebellum Black Coeds at Oberlin College." *Women's Studies Newsletter* 7, no.2 (Spring 1979): 8-11.

Reports preliminary findings of research on the history of black women students at Oberlin College.

68. Higginbotham, Elizabeth. "Race and Class Barriers to Black Women's College Attendance." *Journal of Ethnic Studies* 13, no.1 (Spring 1985): 89-107.

Examines the ways in which socio-economic class affects the college experience of black women. The study focuses on the strategies used to obtain a college education and the significance of early socialization. The author concludes that both race and class operate together to either create or limit options for educational attainment for blacks. Lower-class families, lacking financial resources, had to use other strategies to secure an education for their daughters such as teaching them the value of education and insisting on striving for excellence.

69. Hine, Darlene C. "From Hospital to College: Black Nurse Leaders and the Rise of Collegiate Nursing Schools." *Journal of Negro Education* 51, no.3 (Summer 1982): 222-237.

Discusses the efforts of black women leaders in the nursing profession to establish collegiate schools of nursing for black women.

70. Marable, June M. "The Role of Women in Public School Administration as Perceived by Black Women Administrators in the Field." Ph.D. diss., Miami University, 1974.

Researched the status of black women in public school administration by surveying the opinions of 225 black women administrators in seven selected public school districts in Ohio. Participants in the study indicated that non-observance of equal rights for women was the most important factor affecting the status of black women in administration. Race was considered to be less of a problem than gender in hindering advancement.

71. McGinty, Doris E. "Gifted Minds and Pure Hearts: Mary L. Europe and Estelle Pinckney Webster." *Journal of Negro Education* 51, no.3 (Summer 1982): 266-277.

    Profiles the careers of two outstanding black women music teachers who taught in the Washington D.C. public schools in the early years of the twentieth century.

72. Mosley, Myrtis H. "Black Women Administrators in Higher Education: An Endangered Species." *Journal of Black Studies* 10, no.3 (March 1980): 295-310.

    Analyzes the situation of black women administrators in higher education. Says that there are very few black women in administrative positions in institutions of higher education, and their numbers are shrinking. Asserts that affirmative action policies have failed to recruit black women to higher education. In addition, black male colleagues are sometimes jealous and nonsupportive of black women administrators.

73. Perkins, Linda "Heeds Life's Demands: The Educational Philosophy of Fanny Jackson Coppin." *Journal of Negro Education* 51, no.3 (Summer 1982): 181-190.

    Illuminates the contributions of Fanny Jackson Coppin to the education and advancement of blacks. Born a slave in 1837, she was the first black female graduate of Oberlin College. An outstanding teacher, she was also principal for many years of The Institute for Colored Youth in Philadelphia.

74. Perkins, Linda "The Impact of the 'Cult of True Womanhood' on the Education of Black Women." *Journal of Social Issues* 39, no.3 (1983): 17-28.

    Compares the education of black women to that of white women in the nineteenth century. For black women education served as a means to aid the improvement of their race. Unlike white women of the period, marriage and education were not considered incompatible for black women according to Perkins.

75. Pinderhughes, Dianne M. "Black Women and National Educational Policy." *Journal of Negro Education* 51, no.3 (Summer 1982): 301-308.

    Examines the ways in which black women in policy-making positions, such as Shirley Chisholm and Patricia Roberts Harris, have influenced educational policy at the federal level.

76. Reeder, Amy L., and R.D. Conger. "Differential Mother and Father Influences on the Educational Attainment of Black and White Women." *Sociological Quarterly* 25, no.2 (1984): 239-250.

    An empirical study which compared the educational attainment of black women to white women and the impact of maternal and paternal influences on it. Results indicated that there are different patterns in the way mothers and fathers influence their daughters' educational attainment. For black women, the mother's occupation and her expectations for her daughter were more important factors than the father's occupation.

77. Roberts, Vashti B. "Administrative Employment of Black Women in California Public School Districts: 1974, 1976 and 1978." Ed.D. diss., University of Southern California, 1982.

    Investigated employment opportunities for black female public school administrators in California. Looked for patterns of change in Equal Employment Opportunity Commission statistics for 1974, 1976 and 1978. Results indicated that very little change had occurred over this time period. Concluded that opportunities for black female administrators are declining and advancement is limited.

78. Robinson, Omelia T. "Contributions of Black American Academic Women to American Higher Education." Ph.D. diss., Wayne State University, 1978.

    This study had two purposes: 1. to compile a list of black women who have made a significant contribution to higher education, and 2. to study contemporary black female educators employed in academic institutions. Concludes that since 1970 an increased number of Afro-American women have been appointed as professors and administrators in academic institutions.

79. Royster-Horn, Juana R. "The Academic and Extra-Curricular Undergraduate Experiences of Three Black Women at the University of Washington 1935 to 1941." Ph.D. diss., University of Washington, 1980.

    This study used the oral history approach to examine the experiences of three black college women who attended the University of Washington between 1935 and 1941. Author found that although the women had positive experiences they had been subjected to some sexist and ethnic discrimination. All three women had positive family and community support which enabled them to succeed in completing college.

80. Smith, Carol H. "Black Female Achievers in Academe." *Journal of Negro Education* 51, no.3 (Summer 1982): 318-341.

Highlights the achievements of fifteen black women administrators whom the author believes have made an impact in higher education through their leadership roles. Points out that through hard work and perseverance these women were successful in achieving their goals in spite of racial and gender discrimination.

81. Smith, Glenda D. "Black Women in Continuing Education: The Effects of Socio-Economic Status and Various Psychosocial Variables at Specific Functions Within the Innovation-Decision Process." Ed.D. diss., Temple University, 1977.

Analyzed the characteristics of a group of mature, part-time, black, female students at Cheyney State College to survey their needs regarding counseling, programming and recruitment. Fifty percent of the women were single, heads of households. They showed high determination to complete college. Results of the study determined that more diffusion of information concerning continuing education opportunities is needed in black communities.

82. Swann, Ruth N., and Elaine P. Witty. "Black Women Administrators at Traditional Black Colleges and Universities: Attitudes, Perceptions, and Potentials." *Western Journal of Black Studies* 4, no.4 (Winter 1980): 261-270.

Examines the problems, prospects, and coping strategies of Afro-American women administrators in traditionally black institutions of higher education. Surveyed the opinions of 116 women.

83. Tobin, McLean. *The Black Female Ph.D: Education and Career Development.* Washington, D.C.: University Press of America, 1981.

Analyzed the patterns of career development among black women doctorate holders employed at predominately black public colleges and universities. Author found that most black women Ph.D.'s are concentrated in the field of education. Recommends that young black women be encouraged to enter non-traditional fields.

84. Wade, Ernest M. "Comparative Analysis of Counselor Response to Married and Single Black Female Parents in Terms of Acceptance, Effective Parenting, and the Need for Further Counseling." Ph.D. diss., Michigan State University, 1983.

Tested the response and perceptions of school counselors to black, female-headed, single-parent families by comparing them with black two-parent families.

85.   Wehrle, James M. "The Marriage Squeeze: Perceptions and
      Adaptations of Black Female Doctorates." Ph.D. diss., Southern
      Illinois University at Carbondale, 1982.

      Says that there are more highly educated black females than
      black males. Thus, it is difficult for educated black women to
      marry a black man of comparable status. A nationally-based,
      non-random sample of 224 black female doctorates was surveyed
      to determine how highly educated black women reacted to this
      situation. Subjects coped in a variety of ways such as choosing
      to remain single, postponing marriage, marrying outside their
      race, and marrying men with lower educational attainment.

86.   Whitted, Christine. "Supports in the Black Community: Black
      Unmarried Mothers Who Kept Their Babies and Achieved Their
      Educational and/or Professional Goals." Ph.D. diss., Columbia
      Teachers College, 1978.

      An exploratory, descriptive study with emphasis on the emotional
      and material supports which helped the subjects achieve their
      goals. Tape recorded interviews were conducted with ten women
      between the ages of thirteen and twenty-two who bore children
      out-of-wedlock. These women were able to keep their babies
      and remain in school in order to achieve their professional goals
      because they received support from family, friends or school
      personnel.

Employment

87.   Albelda, Randy P. "Black and White Women Workers in the Post-
      World War II Period." Ph.D. diss., University of Massachusetts,
      1983.

      Examines various theories such as Neo-Classical and Marxist
      concerning the labor force participation of black women during
      the past thirty years. Confirms that racial discrimination
      against black working women does exist.

88.   Allen, Walter R. "Family Roles, Occupational Status, and
      Achievement Orientations Among Black Women in the United
      States." *Signs: Journal of Women in Culture and Society* 4, no.4
      (Summer 1979): 670-686.

      Uses census data to study differences in the occupational
      statuses of black women, black men, white women, and white
      men. Compares achievement orientations of a group of young
      black women just entering the work world to the occupational
      status of black women. Concludes that black females'
      orientation toward achievement is not matched by their probable
      occupational status attainments. States that Afro-American

women in the future are likely to be disproportionately represented in menial, low-paying, low-prestige occupations.

89. Allen, Walter R. "The Social and Economic Statuses of Black Women in the United States." *Phylon* 42, no.1 (March 1981): 26-40.

Analyzes demographic statistics concerning educational attainments, marital and fertility patterns, labor force participation and health status of black females. Concludes that Afro-American women receive lower earnings than white females and males at comparable educational and occupational levels. States that black women are more disadvantaged in total than either blacks as a group or women alone. Says they are consistently undereducated, underpaid, unemployed, victims of marital dissolution and in poorer health than white women or males.

90. Amitin, Kenneth G. "A Correlational Analysis of Selected Career Development Competencies and Personality Characteristics Among Low-Income Black Women." Ph.D. diss., Georgia State University-College of Education, 1978.

A study which measured the relationship between competence in career planning and attainment of career goals. The subjects were low-income black females between the ages of eighteen and forty-four. Results indicated that career planning does lead to attainment of career goals.

91. Anderson, Karen T. "Last Hired, First Fired: Black Women Workers During World War II." *Journal of American History* 69, no.1 (1982): 82-97.

Argues that during the Second World War women of color experienced some upward mobility, but that their position in the American economy basically remained the same by the end of the war. Cites numerous instances of discriminatory practices in hiring black women for work in wartime industries.

92. Ayella, Mary, and John B. Williamson. "The Social Mobility of Women: A Causal Model of Socio-Economic Success." *Sociological Quarterly* 17 (Autumn 1976): 534-554.

A statistical study of heads of households which compares white men, black men, white females, and black females. The data suggests that women's economic success is determined by their educational background, occupation, and race more so than is true for men. Concludes that even with increased education and higher occupational statuses, women do not obtain incomes as high as men with similar educational backgrounds and occupations. Says that this is even more true in the case of black women, therefore, change is needed in the social structure to equalize opportunities for females and blacks.

93. Beckett, Joyce O. "Working Women: A Historical Review of Racial Differences." *The Black Sociologist* 9 (Spring-Summer 1982): 5-27.

A comparative study of black and white women's employment activity from the turn of the century to the 1970s. Concludes that the patterns of employment activity of black women and white women have been different because of the impact of race. Says that until the Civil Rights Acts of the 1960s, black women were excluded from many types of work. Even though progress has been made, black women still continue to hold lower-level positions, to have more unemployment, and to receive lower pay than white women.

94. Bell, Patricia A., and Sara R. Williams. "Black Women's Participation in the Labor Force." *Free Inquiry in Creative Sociology* 9, no.2 (November 1981): 159-161.

Maintains that there are other factors in addition to economic necessity which motivate black wives to enter the work force. The majority of women in this study were committed to working even if by some chance they were able to get enough money to live comfortably without working.

95. Bell-Scott, Patricia. "Preparing Black Women for Nontraditional Professions: Some Considerations for Career Counseling." *Journal of the National Association for Women Deans, Administrators and Counselors*, 40, no.4 (Summer 1977): 135-139.

Asserts that counselors must discard stereotypes of black women and become sensitive to the way in which race, class, sex, and culture might influence the counseling process. Gives recommendations and strategies for increasing the career counselor's awareness and insight of the needs of women of color.

96. Bianchi, Suzanne. *Household Composition and Racial Inequality.* New Brunswick, New Jersey: Rutgers University Press, 1981.

This is a comparative study of the income levels of black and white families. Hypothesizes that economic well-being and family structure are linked. Uses two measures of economic well-being to assess the trend in racial inequality for the 1960-1976 period. Identifies two major shifts in living arrangements which characterize the period of the study: 1. an increase in persons living alone, and 2. the growth of female-headed households with children with the latter factor being more prevalent for blacks than for whites.

97. Brown, Minnie M. "Black Women in American Agricultural History." *Agricultural History* 50, no.1 (1976): 202-212.

The theme of this article is that black women have been an important component of agricultural labor and have made a significant contribution to the development of American agriculture. Notes instances of black women farming on their own without the assistance of men.

98. Brown, Scott C. "Migrants and Workers in Philadelphia: 1850 to 1880." Ph.D. diss., University of Pennsylvania, 1981.

Studied trends and differentials in labor force participation, occupational structure and socio-economic status by sex, race, and place of birth using the Philadelphia population. Sources of data were the census returns for 1850, 1860, 1870, and 1880. Particularly concerned with the impact of technological change on the labor force. Says black women, especially, were placed in a disadvantaged position.

99. Brown, Sherlon P. "Black Awareness and the Career Aspirations and Career Expectations of Black Female High School Seniors." Ph.D. diss., University of Toledo, 1984.

This study tested the relationship between black awareness and the career aspirations of 104 randomly selected black female high school seniors. Outcome indicated there was no positive correlation between Afro-American awareness and career aspirations and expectations.

100. Burlew, Ann K. "The Experiences of Black Females in Traditional and Nontraditional Professions." *Psychology of Women Quarterly* 6, no.3 (Spring 1982): 312-326.

Examined differences in the backgrounds, attitudes, and career expectations of 147 black female undergraduates preparing for careers in traditional and nontraditional professions. Outcome of the study showed that the mothers of the students pursuing nontraditional careers (science, law, engineering) were better educated and were more likely to have worked in non-traditional fields themselves.

101. Burnham, Linda. "Has Poverty Been Feminized in Black America?" *The Black Scholar,* 16, no. 2 (March/April 1985): 14-24.

Argues that the "feminization of poverty" phrase used by feminists presents a highly distorted picture of the dynamics of poverty in the United States because it does not take into consideration the factors of class and race which also contribute to poverty among women of color.

102. Chester, Nia L. "Sex Differentiation in Two High School Environments: Implications for Career Development Among Black Adolescent Females." *Journal of Social Issues* 39, no.3 (1983): 29-40.

Examined interest in male-dominated careers, career aspiration level, maturity of vocational self-concept, and specificity of career plans of 127 black male and female high school students. Students in the study were from two different schools: 1. an integrated vocational high school, and 2. a predominately white liberal arts high school. The results showed that girls at both schools were less interested in male-dominated careers than were the boys, and the liberal arts high school atmosphere was more discouraging to the career development of the black females than to the black males.

103. Christian, Virgil L., and Robert H. Stroup. "The Effect of Education on Related Earnings of Black and White Women." *Economics of Education Review* 1, no.1 (Winter 1981): 113-122.

Compares census data taken from a sample of large southern metropolitan statistical areas of fully employed black and white females in the same labor market and who had comparable levels of education. Results indicate that younger black women in southern cities have closed much of the education gap and are closer to white women in marketable skills. The author specculates that this may be due to the impact of the Civil Rights Acts upon southern employers.

104. Derby, Doris A. "Black Women Basket Makers: A Study of Domestic Economy in Charleston County, South Carolina." Ph.D. Diss., University of Illinois at Urbana-Champaign, 1980.

A study of the economic and artistic activity of basket making in the community of Mount Pleasant, South Carolina.

105. Dill, Bonnie T. "'The Means to Put My Children Through': Child-Rearing Goals and Strategies Among Black Female Domestic Servants." in *The Black Woman*. Edited by La Frances Rodgers-Rose. Beverly Hills, Calif.: Sage Publications, 1979, pp. 107-123.

Used the life history approach to study black women employed as domestic servants. Interviews were conducted with twenty-six black women employed as workers in private households.

The purpose of the study was to explore the relationship between the work of these women and their own families. Most of the women identified education as the primary means to achieve upward mobility for their children, and many of them were aided by their employers in achieving this goal.

106. Dixon-Altenor, Carolyn, and Aiden Altenor. "The Role of Occupational Status in the Career Aspirations of Black Women." *Vocational Guidance Quarterly* 25 (March 1977): 211-216.

Reports the findings of a preliminary investigation of the variables that influence the career decision-making process of black college women. Fifteen black women undergraduate students were asked to rank twenty-five occupations on the basis of perceived salary potential and social status. Subjects' responses in this sample differed significantly from previous studies, and further research in this area is recommended.

107. Fadoyomi, Theophilus O. "Black Women in the Labor Force: An Investigation of factors Affecting the Labor Force Participation of Black Women in the United States." Ph.D. diss., University of Pennsylvania, 1977.

Investigated the differing patterns of labor force participation by white and black women and the major factors influencing it. Confirmed some of the findings of previous research, and concluded that black women continue to work when they marry and have children at a higher rate than do white women.

108. George, Valerie D. "An Investigation of the Occupational Aspirations of Talented Black Adolescent Females." Ph.D. diss., Case Western Reserve University, 1979.

Investigated the career aspirations of sixty-four sophomore high school girls, of whom half were black and half were white. The subjects were all talented students who volunteered for the study. The groups were matched as to socio-economic status. Revealed that race had little to do with occupational aspirations or fear of success. Determined that socio-economic status of the subject's family was a more significant factor.

109. Gilkes, Cheryl T. "Going Up for the Oppressed: The Career Mobility of Black Women Community Workers." *Journal of Social Issues* 39, no.3 (Fall 1983): 115-139.

This article is based on interviews with twenty-five community workers who had public reputations for activism in the black community. Describes how these women developed their careers in a way that was beneficial to the black community as well as to themselves.

110. Gilkes, Cheryl T. "Successful Rebellious Professionals: The Black
      Woman's Professional Identity and Community Commitment."
      Psychology of Women Quarterly 6, no. 3 (Spring 1982): 289-311.

      Discusses the careers of seven professional women, part of a
      larger sample of twenty-five black women community workers.
      This study, based on taped interviews, focuses on successful
      professionals who have achieved success without losing sight of
      the needs of the black community. As administrators of social,
      public, or educational agencies they have had to rebel against
      practices of the dominant society which violate their
      commitment to the needs of people of color.

111. Goldin, Claudia. "Female Labor Force Participation: the Origin of
      Black And White Differences, 1870-1880." *Journal of Economic
      History* 37, no.1 (March 1977): 87-108.

      Analyzes census figures for employed black and white women
      from the census of 1870 and 1880. Concludes that black married
      women participated in the labor force almost six times the rate
      of married white females. Says that black women were largely
      employed in unskilled jobs. Goldin believes the difference
      between the two groups of women can be attributed indirectly
      to the legacy of slavery.

112. Hamburger, Robert. *A Stranger in the House.* New York:
      Macmillan, 1978.

      A collection of narratives of twelve black women employed as
      domestics in the New York area. Based on interviews with the
      women.

113. Harley, Sharon. "Black Women In a Southern City: Washington
      D.C., 1890-1920." in *Sex, Race, and the Role of Women in the
      South.* Edited by Joanne V. Hawks, and Sheila L. Skemp.
      Jackson, Miss.: University Press of Mississippi, 1983, pp. 59-74.

      Concludes that during the period of this study black women
      could find jobs only in semi-skilled and unskilled job categories
      serving as maids, servants, cleaning women and waitresses.
      Says that the lives of Afro-American women were harder than
      any other group. For them the fight to end racial
      discrimination took first place over fighting discrimination based
      on gender.

114. Harley, Sharon. "Northern Black Female Workers: Jacksonian Era."
      in *The Afro-American Woman: Struggles and Images.* Edited by
      Sharon Harley and Rosalyn Terborg-Penn. Port Washington,
      N.Y.: Kennikat Press, 1978, pp. 5-16.

Asserts that Jacksonian egalitarian rhetoric was limited to white males and did not include blacks and females. Moreover, free black women were excluded from factory work and relegated to low paying positions as servants and laundresses.

115. Harrison, Algea O. "Interrole Conflict, Coping, Strategies, and Role Satisfaction Among Single and Married Employed Mothers." *Psychology of Women Quarterly* 6, no.3 (Spring 1982): 354-360.

Studied role conflict in black, nonprofessional women. Found that single mothers were more satisfied with their roles as workers than married mothers.

116. Helmbold, Lois R. "Making Choices, Making Do: Black and White Working Class Women's Lives and Work During the Great Depression." Ph.D. diss., Stanford University, 1983.

A study of the impact of the Depression and its varying effects on the daily life of black and white working class women. Based on interviews conducted by The Women's Bureau in the 1930s with clerical and service workers from Chicago, Cleveland, Philadelphia, and South Bend.

117. Higginbotham, Elizabeth. "Laid Bare by the System: Work and Survival for Black and Hispanic Women." in *Class, Race, and Sex: The Dynamics of Control.* Edited by Amy Swerdlow, and Hanna Lessinger. Boston: G.K. Hall, 1983, pp. 200-215.

Examines the general employment situation of black and Hispanic women in the United States with respect to differences and similarities of the two groups. Says that black women currently have higher levels of educational attainment than Hispanic women, and black women in recent years have used higher education as a means of escaping domestic service.

118. Hine, Darlene C. "The Ethel Johns Report: Black Women in the Nursing Profession, 1925." *Journal of Negro History* 67, no.3 (1982): 212-228.

An historical study of the status of black women in the nursing profession in the 1920s. Says nurse trainees were subjected to inferior training schools, low salaries, professional exclusion, and racist attitudes.

119. Hoffman, Emily P. "Comparative Labor Supply of Black and White Women." *Review of Black Political Economy* 11 (Summer 1982): 429-439.

Investigates the higher labor force participation rate of black women as compared to white women. Also looks at the impact of young children on women's labor force participation rates. Results indicate that the presence of young children deters white women from remaining in the labor force to a greater extent than it does for black women. Also says that white women reduce their hours of work when their husband's incomes increase to a greater extent than do black married women.

120.   Janiewski, Dolores E. *Sisterhood Denied: Race, Gender, and Class in a New South Community*. Philadelphia: Temple University Press, 1985.

A history of the involvement of women in unionizing the tobacco and textile industries in Durham, North Carolina in the 1930s. Examines the complex relationship between race, gender, and class as it was affected by industrialization in this community. Uses oral history, written documents, and census data interpreted by quantitative analysis. As the title implies, Janiewski found that racial differences among the women involved in the labor movement were never completely overcome, but some progress toward solidarity was achieved.

121.   Jones, Beverly W. "Race, Sex, and Class: Black Female Tobacco Workers in Durham, North Carolina, 1920-1940, and the Development of Female Consciousness." *Feminist Studies* 10, no.3 (Fall 1984): 441-451.

This is a study of black female workers in the Durham, North Carolina tobacco industry of the 1920s and 1930s. It is based on interviews with fifteen former employees. Concludes that black women workers were paid the lowest wages, given the worst jobs and confined to separate work areas apart from white female employees. States that this management practice prohibited the formation of gender bonds between black and white working class women.

122.   Jones, Jacqueline. *Labor of Love, Labor of Sorrow: Black Women, Work, and the Family from Slavery to the Present*. New York: Basic Books, 1985.

A narrative survey of black women's roles in the South as workers and family members based on slave narratives, oral histories, diaries, and secondary sources. Particularly noteworthy are the numerous photographs from the National Archives, the New York Public Library, and The Library of Congress.

123.   Katz, Mitchell H., and Chaya S. Piotrkowski. "Correlates of Family Role Strain Among Employed Black Women." *Family Relations* 32, no.3 (July 1983): 331-340.

Tested a sample of fifty-one employed black mothers. Married women with children reported the most role conflict while unmarried women reported the least. Found that the number of children in a family appeared to contribute more to role strain than presence or absence of a husband.

124. Katzman, David M. "White Mistress and Black Servant." Chap. 5. in *Seven Days a Week: Women and Domestic Service in Industrializing America*. New York: Oxford University Press, 1978, pp. 184-222.

Says that domestic service in the post-Civil War South was part of the racial cast structure.

125. Kilson, Marion. "Black Women in the Professions, 1890-1970." *Monthly Labor Review* 100 (May 1977): 38-41.

A brief article which examines census data on black women in the professions. Says they are concentrated in teaching, nursing, and social work, but they participate more in prestigious professions such as law and medicine than do other women.

126. King, Allan G. "Labor Market Racial Discrimination Against Black Women." *Review of Black Political Economy* 8, no.4 (Summer 1978): 325-335.

Asserts that black professional women working in the public sector have achieved virtual earnings parity with white women, but says it cannot be concluded that they do not suffer racial discrimination.

127. Leashore, Bogart R. "Black Female Workers: Live-in Domestics in Detroit, Michigan, 1860-1880." *Phylon* 45, no.2 (June 1984): 111-120.

A study of black female, live-in domestic servants employed in white households in late nineteenth-century Detroit. Based on census data collected for the years 1860, 1870, and 1880. Determines that domestic service for women of color was rooted in racism and sexism.

128. Leggon, Cheryl B. "Black Female Professionals: Dilemmas and Contradictions of Status." in *The Black Woman*. Edited by La Frances Rodgers-Rose. Beverly Hills, Calif.: Sage Pubs., 1980, pp. 189-202.

The thesis of this study is that black female professionals share unique problems because of their dual minority status based on their race and sex. Women in law, medicine, and business were

questioned as to whether gender or race posed a greater
obstacle in the advancement of their career. Results indicated
that the subjects experienced more racial discrimination than
sexual discrimination, and the black movement was more
important to them than the women's movement. Also concluded
that black women view work as obligatory and experience less
role conflict than their white counterparts.

129.   Malson, Michelene R. "Black Women's Sex Roles: The Social
       Context for a New Ideology." *Journal of Social Issues* 39, no.3
       (1983): 101-113.

       Reports the findings of a study in progress which investigates
       the ability of black women to combine the roles of mother and
       homemaker with paid work outside the home. Fifty-four urban
       black women were interviewed of whom the majority were
       employed full-time. All the women who were interviewed were
       responsible for child care and household chores. The author
       concludes that black women do not see employment and
       homemaking as mutually exclusive roles. The mothers of a
       majority of the participants had worked and, thus, served as
       role models for their daughters. Found that role conflicts were
       not internalized, but coping strategies such as child-rearing
       support networks were utilized.

130.   Mednick, Martha T., and Gwendolyn R. Puryear. "Motivational and
       Personality Factors Related to Career Goals of Black Women."
       Journal of Social and Behavioral Sciences 20 (Winter 1975):
       1-30.

       A frequently cited study which examines the level of
       innovativeness of black college women's career choices. Both
       groups of women, those choosing traditional women's careers and
       those choosing nontraditional occupations, expressed little
       conflict between career and marriage goals. Women who chose
       non-traditional careers selected from a wide variety of
       occupational choices, aspired to a higher level of accom-
       plishment, and expressed greater commitment to their fields than
       non-innovators.

131.   Morrison, Gwendolyn C.C. "Characteristics of black females in
       Administrative/Management Level Employment." Ph.D. diss.,
       Texas Woman's University, 1981.

       A descriptive study of fifty-two black female executives.
       Looked at the relationship between annual salary, job
       satisfaction, number of personnel supervised and so forth.

132. Obleton, Nettie B. "Career Choice Among Black Professional Women in Selected Nontraditional Careers." Ph.D. diss., Arizona State University, 1984.

An exploratory study of the factors influencing the career development of black professional women in nontraditional careers (science, engineering, and medicine). Compares these experiences to black women in the traditional career of nursing. Most of the professional women identified an influential person, belief, or circumstance as instrumental in their choice of career. The scientists/engineers said math instructors were the most influential persons affecting their choice of career.

133. Obleton, Nettie B. "Career Counseling Black Women in a Predominantly White Coeducational University." *Personnel and Guidance Journal* 62, no.6 (February 1984): 365-368.

Describes a new technique, the Model-Mentor Process, whereby black female students in predominantly white coeducational universities are matched with black career women in order to encourage and support educational and career goals of black women students.

134. Pearce, Diana M. "The Feminization of Ghetto Poverty." *Society* 21 (November-December 1983): 70-74.

Asserts that there is a new kind of schism in black America. Families headed by women are becoming poorer, while black two-parent families are increasing their economic status. States that black women experience quantitatively more poverty than white women because of the dual impact of racial and gender discrimination. Says that black women are bearing the burden of poverty in the black community.

135. Puryear, Gwendolyn R. "The Black Woman: Liberated or Oppressed?." in *Comparative Perspectives of Third World Women*. Edited by Beverly Lindsay. New York: Praeger, 1980, pp. 251-275.

Summarizes the findings of primary research studies. Argues that the black woman holds no favored position in the labor market and, therefore, cannot be considered liberated. States that Afro-American women must work out of economic necessity, and there are more unemployed black women than any other group. Adds that women of color are underrepresented in the professions and tend to be concentrated in the traditional female fields of nursing and teaching.

136. Ramos, Marcia C. "A Study of Black Women in Management." Ed.D. diss., University of Massachusetts, 1981.

Uses a life period development model to describe the career development of black women managers. Uses a structural interview schedule to conduct intensive interviews with ten black male and ten black female managers. Results of the study did not indicate any sex related differences between the two groups of subjects.

137.   Rexroat, Cynthia. "The Changing Cost of Being a Black Woman." *Sociology of Work and Occupations* 5, no.3 (August 1978): 341-358.

Compares the economic position of black women who work full-time, year-round to white women using census data from 1960 and 1970. Found that black women had improved their economic status during the period of the 1960s. The economic difference between white and black women had narrowed considerably between 1960 and 1970 which is attributed to increased educational attainment for women of color and to civil rights legislation.

138.   Rogers, Laura S. "Locus of Control, Vocational Exploratory Behavior, and Career Choices of Black Women." Ed.D. diss., Rutgers University, 1984.

Evaluates the relationship between nontraditional and traditional career choice and personal characteristics of ninety-five black women students in an urban community college. Outcome of the study was inconclusive.

139.   Rollins, Judith. *Between Women: Domestics and Their Employers.* Philadelphia: Temple University Press, 1985.

Examines the relationship between black domestics and their white female employers. Rollins believes this is a unique arrangement between employee and employer because both are females. She conducted in-depth interviews with twenty employers and twenty domestics and also worked as a servant herself for ten employers. She observed that domestics are treated as if they were invisible and concludes that the relationship between domestics and their employers serves to maintain a class structure based on racial and economic inequality.

140.   Simpson, Gwyned. "The Daughters of Charlotte Ray: The Career Development Process During the Exploratory and Establishment Stages of Black Women Attorneys." *Sex Roles* 11, no.1-2 (July 1984): 113-139.

Studies black women in the legal profession. Fifteen black women lawyers were interviewed in order to determine factors

which influenced their career decisions. Educational values in
the home, economic resources of the family, significant role
models, affirmative action policies, and minority recruitment
programs contributed to the subjects' decision to enter the
profession of law.

141. Simpson, Wessylyne A. "Self Concept and Career Choice Among
Black Women." Ed.D. diss., Oklahoma State University, 1975.

A correlational study of the relationship between self-concept
and career choice of Afro-American women. The sample
included fifty college women, fifty high school girls who in-
tended to enter college, and fifty high school girls who did not
plan to attend college. No relationship between self-concept
and career choice was found.

142. Smith, Elsie J. "The Black Female Adolescent: A Review of the
Educational, Career and Psychological Literature." *Psychology of
Women Quarterly* 6, no.3 (Spring 1982): 261-288.

Summarizes research in the area of educational, career, and
psychological development of black female adolescents.
Recommends that more attention should be devoted to analyzing
the role of the family and parents' influence on the educational
and occupational aspirations of Afro-American female
adolescents.

143. Taylor, Norma J. "Occupational Choices of Black Women: A
Longitudinal Study of Two Cohorts." Ph.D. diss., The F. Heller
Graduate School for Advanced Studies in Social Work, 1984.

A longitudinal survey which investigated the labor market
experiences of two groups of black women over a ten year
period. Taylor found that despite some gains, Afro-American
women still had not penetrated the high-paying, high-status
occupations in significant numbers.

144. Wallace, Phyllis A. *Black Women in the Labor Force*. Cambridge,
Mass.: MIT Press, 1980.

Surveys recent economic research on the subject of black
working women. Focuses on the period after 1960. Includes
chapters on characteristics of black women workers, earnings,
special groups such as teenagers, and the effects of training
programs and anti-discrimination efforts to alleviate
unemployment. Concludes that the negative effects of racial
discrimination in employment have not been offset by gains in
education and improved employment opportunities as a result of
training programs and the like.

145.   White, Felicia T. "A Description of the Educational Attainment,
       Occupational Status, and Aspirations of Young Black Women
       from the High School Class of 1972." Ph.D. diss., University of
       Maryland, 1981.

       Studied economic and class differences of young black women in
       the labor force. Outcome of the investigation indicated that
       there are significant differences between classes with regard to
       educational and occupational attainment and level of aspiration
       with women from wealthier families having higher aspirations.

146.   Wright, Maggie S. "Parent-Child Relations, Achievement
       Motivation, and Sex Role Attitudes Among Black and White
       Professional Women in Traditional and Pioneer Occupations."
       Ph.D. diss., State University of New York at Buffalo, 1981.

       A study of 185 black and white professional working women in
       the United States which found that frequency of choice of a
       non-traditional or pioneer career is related to the masculine sex
       role and levels of education attained for black professional
       women.

147.   Zukerman, Diana M. "Sex-Role Related Goals and Attitudes of
       Minority Students: A Study of Black College Women and Reentry
       Students." *Journal of College Student Personnel* 22, no.1
       (January 1981): 23-30.

       Assesses the sex-related goals and attitudes of reentry students
       and black female undergraduate students. Questions asked
       concerned educational and career goals, career commitment,
       feminist attitudes and family background. Results indicated a
       majority of the Afro-American women plan nontraditional
       careers, and eighty-three percent of the black women prefer
       full-time careers.

Feminism and Women's Studies

148.   Almquist, Elizabeth M. "Black Women and the Pursuit of Equality."
       in *Women: A Feminist Perspective.* 2d ed. Edited by Jo
       Freeman. Palo Alto, Calif.: Mayfield Publishing Co., 1977, pp.
       430-451.

       Asserts that black women do support the women's movement.
       Attempts to demonstrate that black women and white women
       have similar problems such as the fact that they both are
       victims of sexual discrimination. Says that sexual discrimination
       rather than racial discrimination accounts for lower salaries of
       black women.

149. Almquist, Elizabeth M. "Untangling the Effects of Race and Sex: the Disadvantaged Status of Black Women." *Social Science Quarterly* 56, no.1 (June 1975): 129-142.

     This is a rejoinder to the article by Mae King appearing in the same issue (see item 171). Uses a statistical model to gauge the effects of race and sex and to determine which is a greater handicap to black women. Results of her study support the hypothesis that sex-based gaps in income exceed race-based gaps in income. Thus, she concludes that sexual discrimination is more detrimental to black women than racial discrimination. Believes that women cannot afford to be divided along racial lines.

150. Andolsen, Barbara H. *Daughters of Jefferson, Daughters of Bootblacks*. Macon, Georgia: Mercer University Press, 1986.

     Focuses on the intertwining of racism and sexism within the women's movement. The first four chapters discuss racism in the nineteenth-century women's suffrage movement. Chapter five analyzes contemporary perspectives of black women on feminism. Written by a middle-class white woman who believes white feminists need to learn about the perspectives of black women in order to begin a dialogue about issues important to all women.

151. Avakian, Arlene V. "Women's Studies and Racism." *New England Journal of Black Studies* 1 (1981): 31-36.

     Says that the concerns of black women are omitted from women's studies courses.

152. Beal, Francis M. "Slave of a Slave No More: Black Women in Struggle." *Black Scholar* 6, no.6 (March 1975): 16-24.

     Asserts that black women are exploited by black men. Urges Afro-American women to combat the causes of racism and sexism. Beal writes from a Marxist perspective, and she believes that class exploitation is more significant than racial or sexual oppression.

153. Bulkin, Elly et al. *Yours in Struggle: Three Feminist Perspectives on Anti-semitism and Racism*. Brooklyn, New York: Long Haul Press, 1984.

     These are intensely personal reflections written in an informal conversational tone on the subject of racism, sexism and anti-semitism in the lives of three women who come from very differerent cultures. All three are lesbian feminists. One was raised in the South as a white Christian. The second author is

an Afro-American, and the third is an Ashkenazi Jew. They
have cooperated on this book as way of building coalitions
between women of different races and creeds.

154. Butler, Johnella E. et al. "Black Studies and Women's Studies:
      Search for a Long Overdue Partnership." *Women's Studies
      Quarterly* 10, no.2 (Summer 1982): 10-16.

      Advocates establishing a relationship between black studies and
      women's studies. Says that before this can be done, racism in
      women's studies scholarship must be overcome, and the male bias
      in black studies must be changed. The study of black women
      must be based on a partnership between the disciplines of black
      studies and women's studies. Says women of color have been
      ignored too long by both disciplines.

155. Cole, Jonnetta B. "Black Women as Colleagues in Black Studies."
      New England Journal of Black Studies 1 (1981): 3-8.

      Outlines some of the ways black women are discriminated
      against by male colleagues in black studies programs. Says that
      there are very few black women in leadership positions in the
      field of black studies.

156. Dill, Bonnie T. "'On the Hem of Life': Race, Class, and the
      Prospects for Sisterhood." in *Class, Race, and Sex: The
      Dynamics of Control.* Edited by Amy Swerdlow and Hanna
      Lessinger. Boston: G.K. Hall, 1983, pp. 173-188.

      Analyzes the relationship of race, class and patriarchal sex
      hierarchy on the concept of sisterhood between women of
      different races, and reviews some of the literature on the
      subject. States that women must recognize and accept our
      differences, but attempt to build coalitions around issues of
      shared interest.

157. Dill, Bonnie T. "Race, Class, and Gender: Prospects for an All-
      Inclusive Sisterhood." *Feminist Studies* 9, no.1 (Spring 1983):
      130-149.

      Examines the concept of sisterhood in the contemporary women's
      movement. Concludes that the differences between black women
      and white women, working-class and middle-class women are too
      deep-rooted to permit an all-inclusive sisterhood. Dill
      recommends abandoning the above concept and substituting a
      pluralistic approach which concentrates on coalition building
      based on shared interests.

158. Eichelberger, Brenda. "Voices on Black Feminism." *Quest* 3, no.4
      (Spring 1977): 16-28.

This study is based on interviews with eight black women sharing common interests in black feminism. Reasons given for nonparticipation in the women's movement include: class differences, society's negative image of the black woman and the black woman's own negative self-image, negative public image of the women's movement, lack of knowledge about the movement, and racist attitudes of white feminists. Concludes that there is a need for black feminism because black women must speak for themselves.

159. Fisher, Beverly. "Race and Class: Beyond Personal Politics." *Quest* 3, no.4 (Spring 1977): 2-15.

This article is written for white feminist readers in an attempt to illuminate reasons why the women's movement has failed to understand the perspective of women of color and working-class women. Based on interviews with three women active in the National Congress of Neighborhood Women in Brooklyn, New York. Informants give their impressions of the white, middle-class women's movement and reasons for not joining it.

160. Gilkes, Cheryl T. "From Slavery to Social Welfare: Racism and the Control of Black Women." in *Class, Race, and Sex: The Dynamics of Control*. Edited by Amy Swerdlow and Hanna Lessinger. Boston: G.K. Hall, 1983, pp. 288-300.

Although historically black women have been feminists in their ideals and philosophy, Gilkes' believes the fight against racism is still the principal struggle for black women. She states that the rise of the "New Right" represented by the Reagan administration may intensify the existing racial divisions among women.

161. Hemmons, Willa M. "The Women's Liberation Movement: Understanding Black Women's Attitudes." in *The Black Woman*. Edited by La Frances Rodgers-Rose. Beverly Hills, Calif.: Sage Publications, 1980, pp. 285-297.

A social psychological investigation of the attitudes of black women towards the women's liberation movement. Based on the author's 1973 dissertation which compared the opinions of forty-five black women and thirty-seven white women. Data showed that black women were not opposed to the ideas and precepts of the women's movement. Although black women were more likely to hold traditional values of femininity, this did not decrease the percentage who showed a positive attitude toward the women's movement.

162. Henry, Charles P., and Francis S. Foster. "Black Women's Studies:
      Threat or Challenge?" *The Western Journal of Black Studies* 6,
      no.1 (Spring 1982): 15-21.

      Traces the origin of black feminism and its relationship with the
      contemporary women's movement, the black power movement,
      and the Marxist-Leninist viewpoint. Argues that black studies
      and women's studies must share their different perspectives in
      order to further the goal of including the study of black women
      in the curriculum. Says that some bridge-building between the
      two perspectives is needed.

163. Higginbotham, Elizabeth. "Issues in Contemporary Sociological Work
      on Black Women." *Humanity and Society* 4, no.3 (November
      1980): 226-242.

      A review essay of sociological and social scientific studies of
      the black woman. The author blames social scientists for
      contributing to the negative image of black women. Says two
      stereotypes of the Afro-American woman are present in the
      social science literature: 1. black women as inadequate, and 2.
      the superwoman image. The author contends that it is
      unrealistic and unfair to ask women of color to choose between
      their race and their sex, and she asserts that black women must
      be fully integrated into women's studies.

164. Hoffman, Nancy. "Black Studies, Ethnic Studies and Women's
      Studies: Some Reflections on Collaborative Projects." *Women's
      Studies Quarterly* 14, no.1 and 2 (Spring/Summer 1986): 49-53.

      Describes the purpose and results of several projects carried out
      in academic institutions across the country designed to integrate
      black studies and women's studies into the curriculum by
      developing new courses and revising old ones.

165. Hood, Elizabeth F. "Black Women, White Women: Separate Paths to
      Liberation." *The Black Scholar* 9, no.7 (April 1978): 45-56.

      Focuses on the reasons why black women and white women
      react differently to the women's movement. Hood feels that
      racial discrimination is more oppressive than discrimination
      based on gender. She says that since white feminists have not
      fought against racism, blacks cannot fight sexism.

166. Hooks, Bell. *Ain't I a Woman: Black Women and Feminism.* Boston:
      South End Press, 1981.

      The primary intent in this work is to document the impact of
      sexism on the social status of black women. Examines the
      impact of sexism on Afro-American women during slavery, the

devaluation of black womanhood, black male sexism, racism within the recent feminist movement, and the black woman's involvement with feminism. Says there is a tendency to equate blacks with black men and the women's movement with white women. Black women are forced to choose between the two movements. Hooks' contends that the two issues of racism and sexism are inseparable, and both issues must be incorporated into the women's liberation movement.

167. Hooks, Bell. *Feminist Theory: From Margin to Center.* Boston: South End Press, 1984.

The premise of this book is that contemporary feminist theory does not include race and class as a form of oppression. Argues that feminism has become a white bourgeois movement, and says feminists need to look beyond sexism as a form of oppression.

168. Hraba, Joseph, and Paul Yarbrough. "Gender Consciousness and Class Action for Women: A Comparison of Black and White Female Adolescents." *Youth and Society* 15, no.2 (December 1983): 115-131.

Surveys the commitment of adolescents to feminist class action and gender consciousness. Compares two samples of high school students: one of black youth and one of white adolescents. Findings indicate that young black women students did not connect the women's movement with commitment to action for women. This study is quite dated since the research was conducted in 1974.

169. Hull, Gloria T. et al. *All the Women Are White, All the Blacks Are Men, But Some of Us Are Brave: Black Women's Studies.* New York: The Feminist Press, 1982.

Designed as a reference text and a pedagogical tool, this work provides examples of recent research and teaching about black women. The first two sections establish the framework for the study of black women from a feminist, anti-racist perspective. Essays in additional chapters are grouped around subtopics such as black women's literature, and black women in social science among others. A large portion is devoted to bibliographies and bibliographic essays. The last section contains sample course syllabi.

170. Joseph, Gloria I. *Common Differences: Conflicts in Black and White Feminist Perspectives.* New York: Anchor Press/Doubleday, 1981.

Examines the ways in which racial and sexual factors interact in the oppression of women. Maintains that coalitions between white women and black women are necessary, but differences between the two groups must be recognized. Says that misinformation has contributed to the black movement viewing feminists with suspicion, and the black community has ignored the question of sexual politics for far too long. This book is a collaborative effort of a black woman and a white woman and is based on three years of dialogue and working through their views.

171. King, Mae. "Oppression and Power: the Unique Status of the Black Woman in the American Political System." *Social Science Quarterly* 56, no.1 (June 1975): 116-128.

Maintains blacks in American society are in an inferior caste not unlike the caste system in India and that this system is rooted in the heritage of slavery. Says that since black women and white women are members of different castes, there can be no alliance between them based on mutual concern with gender discrimination. King believes that race rather than sex is more important as a determinant of the status of black women. Asserts that the political-economic system must change before black women can achieve equality. Says that alliances between black women and white women will not benefit women of color.

172. Lewis, Diane K. "A Response to Inequality: Black Women, Racism, and Sexism." *Signs: Journal of Women in Culture and Society* 3, no.2 (Winter 1977): 339-361.

Maintains that the black liberation movement was more beneficial in generating changes for black males than for black women. Afro-American women experienced increased gender discrimination as they increased their participation in the public sphere. Author analyzes employment statistics to back up her point that black women experience both racial and sexual discrimination. In the last few years women of color have had a more favorable view of the women's movement due to their heightened awareness of gender discrimination in employment.

173. Lorde, Audre. *Sister Outsider.* New York: The Crossing Press, 1984.

A collection of fifteen essays and speeches which articulate Lorde's views regarding black feminism. These are intensely personal writings which reflect the author's experiences as a black, lesbian woman in a racist, sexist society. Says that the goal of sisterhood between black women will not be achieved easily. Black lesbians are caught between racism of white women and homophobia of their black sisters. States that the future of the world may depend on all women learning to relate across their differences and to identify with each other.

174. Manning, Marable. "Groundings With My Sisters: Patriarchy and the Exploitation of Black Women." *Journal of Ethnic Studies* 11 (Summer 1983): 1-39.

    Section I discusses slavery as an economic institution and the central role of black women in maintaining that institution as slave breeders and laborers. Section II focuses on the history of black women as political activists. Section III describes the sexism of males in the black power movement of the 1960s. Asserts that the black protest movement was compromised by its inability to confront the reality of patriarchy.

175. Moraga, Cherie, and Gloria Anzaldua, eds. *This Bridge Called My Back: Writings by Radical Women of Color*. Watertown, Mass.: Persephone Press, 1981.

    An anthology of selections by twenty-nine women of color ranging from stream of consciousness journal entries and poetry to well thought-out theoretical statements. Works by Afro-American, Latina, Native American, and Asian American women are included in this collection. The purpose of this anthology is to call for community and sisterhood among women of all minority groups. The idea for the book stemmed from the alienation the editors felt in the white feminist movement which is reflected in the articles. It is aimed at all women's studies and ethnic studies instructors with the idea that it will serve as a consciousness-raising tool.

176. Nelson, Janie M. "Attitude Behavior Consistency Among Black Feminist and Traditional Black Women." Ph.D. diss., Kent State University, 1981.

    Compared the attitude toward feminism of fifty-four black feminist women and forty-nine traditional black women. Examined the correlation between feminist outlook and assertive behavior in black women. Results indicated a lack of consistency between attitude and assertive behavior of the black feminist women more so than the traditional black woman.

177. Omolade, Barbara. "Black Women and Feminism." in *The Future of Difference*. Edited by Hester Eisenstein and Alice Jordine. Boston: G.K. Hall, 1980.

    Juxtaposes the role of black women in traditional African societies with the role of white women in medieval Europe. Argues that traditional African societies were not patriarchal as were European societies. African women had certain rights and status in society. Maintains that this must be understood by white feminists before a dialogue between black women and white women can take place. Admits that black leaders in the civil rights movement restricted the role of black women. On the other hand, white feminists failed to take a militant stand against racism. Authors make a plea for black women to speak for themselves and for black feminism. A very succinct analysis of the issues involved in the intersection of racism and sexism.

178. Painter, Diann H. "The Black Woman in American Society." *Current History* 70 (May 1976): 224-227,234.

Contends that racism, with its historical roots in the slave system, and the economic insecurity of black families are the reasons for the diferences in the roles of white women in the home and black women in the labor market. Says that black women have not embraced feminism because they are more concerned with the status of all members of their race. Yet, black women are aware that overcoming sexist barriers are necessary in order to have access to increased economic opportunities.

179. Palmer, Phyllis M. "White Women/Black Women: the Dualism of Female Identity and Experience in the United States." *Feminist Studies* 9, no.1 (Spring 1983): 150-170.

This is written from the perspective of a white feminist academic who admits that most writings, including her own, have treated race and class as secondary issues to feminism. She states that black women have been used as symbols for women's liberation at the same time they are criticized for their failure to support the movement.

180. Ransford, H. Edward, and Jon Miller. "Race, Sex and Feminist Outlooks." *American Sociological Review* 48 (February 1983): 46-59.

An empirical study which examines the combination of race, gender, and class in order to explain sex role outlooks of black females, white females, black males, and white males. Hypothesizes that black women will be more sympathetic toward the women's liberation movement because black women have had to work outside the home and thus are more independent and self-reliant than white women. Results of the study did not support the hypothesis.

181. Reid, Pamela T. "Feminism Versus Minority Group Identity: Not for Black Women Only." *Sex Roles* 10, no.3/4 (February 1984): 247-255.

Reviews some of the issues concerning the role of black women and feminism found in recent literature. Identifies four hypotheses found in social science research: black women will weaken the feminist movement because of their concern with racism, the "double whammy" which holds that black women are victims of racial and gender discrimination, the black matriarchy concept, and the idea that sexism is more detrimental to black women than is race. Discusses the implications these hypotheses have for researchers

182. Ruether, Rosemary. "Between the Sons of Whites and the Sons of Blackness: Racism and Sexism in America." Chap. 5 in *New Woman/New Earth: Sexist Ideologies and Human Liberation*. New York: Seabury Press, 1975, pp. 115-133.

Argues that the contemporary women's movement must reach out to oppressed minority groups and include other kinds of oppression such as racial and class oppression as part of its struggle. It must not follow the example of the nineteenth-century women's movement which became a movement to enfranchise middle-class white women at the expense of excluding blacks and immigrants. Points out the existence of sexism in the black movement especially in religious groups such as the Black Muslims where the patriarchal family model is emphasized. Says that this is damaging to black male/female relationships.

183. Simmons, Margaret A. "Racism and Feminism: A Schism in the Sisterhood." *Feminist Studies* 5, no.2 (Summer 1979): 384-401.

Contends that the problem of racism and ethno-centrism in the feminist movement has not been accepted by white feminists. Simmons' critiques the works of major feminist theorists: Simone de Beauvoir's, *The Second Sex*, Robin Morgan's *Sisterhood is Powerful*, Shulamith Firestone's *The Dialectics of Sex*, Kate Millet's *Sexual Politics*, and Mary Daly's *Beyond God the Father*. Asserts that each of these white feminists overlooks the different experiences of minority women, and ethnic women are largely invisible in most contemporary feminist theory.

184. Slane, Steve, and Lisa Morrow. "Race Differences in Feminism and Guilt." *Psychological Reports* 49, no.1 (August 1981): 45-46.

Reports the results of an empirical study which compared the feminist beliefs of black women and white women and related those beliefs to several guilt indices. Results of the study indicated that for black feminists issues of sexuality are less important than the issue of racial equality.

185. Smith, Althea, and Abigail J. Stewart. "Approaches to Studying Racism and Sexism in Black Women's Lives." *Journal of Social Issues* 39, no.3 (1983): 1-15.

Proposes an alternative approach to studying the effects of racism and sexism. Says an interactive, contextual model of racism and sexism is needed. Recommends that more research should be focused on black women and the impact of racism and sexism.

186.   Smith, Barbara. "Some Home Truths On the Contemporary Black Feminist Movement." *Black Scholar* 16 (March-April 1985): 4-13.

Contends that sexism and racism are simultaneous oppressions for women of color and the two issues are of equal importance. Disputes some of the common myths concerning black women and feminism such as the belief that black women are already liberated.

187.   Smith, Barbara, ed. *Home Girls: A Black Feminist Anthology.* New York: Kitchen Table/Women of Color Press, 1983.

Contains fiction, poetry, literary criticism, political analyses, and essays by thirty-four contributors. The primary purpose of this collection is to dispel the myth that black women are already liberated and to make a case for coalition building among feminists of different racial, ethnic, and national groups. It is particularly concerned with homophobia and the exclusion of black lesbians from the women's movement and from the black community. Smith's introduction contains a good overview of the philosophy of black feminism, and a history of black feminism is contained in "The Combahee River Collective Statement."

188.   Spellman, Elizabeth V. "Theories of Race and Gender: the Erasure of Black Women." *Quest* 5, no.4 (1982): 36-59.

Compares views of racism and sexism in recent theoretical works. Sees racism and sexism as interlocking not merely a compounded experience for black women. Refutes the view that sexism is a more fundamental issue than racism. Accuses white women of having tunnel vision when it concerns black women.

189.   Stadler, Quandra P. "Visibility and Difference: Black Women in History and Literature: Pieces of a Paper and Some Ruminations." in *The Future of Difference.* Edited by Hester Eisenstein and Alice Jardine. Boston: G.K. Hall, 1980, pp.239-246.

Believes black women are "natural" feminists because they have always worked outside the home and have looked for personal fulfillment.

190. Stone, Pauline T. "Feminist Consciousness and Black Women." in
     Women: A Feminist Perspective. 2nd ed. Edited by Jo Freeman.
     Palo Alto, Calif.: Mayfield Publishing Co., 1979, pp. 575-588.

     Challenges the view that racism is the major cause for the
     unequal condition of black women in the United States. Argues
     that black women are subjected to the forces of the capitalist
     economy and the sex-segregated labor force to the same extent
     as are white women, therefore black women are victimized by
     both racism and sexism. Believes that the white racist theory
     of a black matriarchy has prevented black women from joining
     the women's movement.

191. Torrey, Jane W. "Racism and Feminism: Is Women's Liberation for
     Whites Only?" *Psychology of Women Quarterly* 4, no.2 (Winter
     1979): 281-293.

     A review of the literature discussing the role of black women
     and the women's movement. Suggests one reason black women
     have not joined white feminist organizations may be because the
     black movement and the feminist movement are in competition
     with each other.

192. Wallace, Michele. *Black Macho and the Myth of the Superwoman*.
     New York: Dial Press, 1979.

     A personal account of the damage done to black women by the
     black power movement and the Moynihan Report which proposed
     the existence of a so-called black matriarchy. It blends auto-
     biography, history, and social and literary analysis. Although it
     does not pretend to be a scholarly work, it is an important book
     because of the criticism and debate its publication produced
     among black scholars and the black community.

193. White, E. Francis. "Listening to the Voices of Black Feminism."
     Radical America 18, no.2-3 (March-June 1984): 7-25.

     An excellent critique of recent theoretical writings by black
     feminists such as Barbara Smith, Bell Hooks and Gloria Josephs.
     White is quick to point out faulty arguments and mis-
     interpretations of history, although essentially she agrees with
     the philosophy of black feminism espoused by the above
     theorists.

194. Williamson, Dorothy K. "Rhetorical Analysis of Selected Modern
     Black American Spokespersons on the Women's Liberation
     Movement." Ph.D. diss., Ohio State University, 1981.

     Analyzes and criticizes the rhetoric of Shirley Chisholm, Toni
     Morrison, and Robert Staples on the current women's movement

in the United States. Williamson found that the three spokes-
persons agree that the women's movement has had an impact
upon the black community, but they disagree as to whether or
not the impact has been positive or negative.

History and Politics

195.   Aptheker, Bettina. "The Suppression of the *Free Speech*: Ida B.
       Wells and the Memphis Lynching." *San Jose Studies* 3 (November
       1977): 34-40.

       Describes events surrounding the lynching of three black men in
       Memphis, Tennessee in 1892, and Ida B. Wells' fight to defend
       them in the pages of her newspaper, *The Free Speech*.

196.   Aptheker, Bettina. *Woman's Legacy: Essays on Race, Sex, and
       Class in American History.* Amherst, Mass.: The University of
       Massachusetts Press, 1982.

       A collection of interpretive essays on the theme of the
       interrelationship between the Afro-American liberation movement
       and the movement to emancipate women. Contends that for
       black women equality is not possible without overcoming both
       racism and male supremacy. Some of the topics discussed are:
       the battle over the Fifteenth Amendment and the abolitionist
       and women's rights movements, the crusade against lynching and
       the women's suffrage movement, W.E.B. DuBois and women's
       emancipation, and the impact of the Moynihan Report.

197.   Armitage, Sue et al. "Black Women and Their Communities in
       Colorado." *Frontiers* 2, 2 (Summer 1977): 45-51.

       Based on oral history excerpts obtained from six black women,
       this article highlights the role women played in black pioneer
       communities in Colorado.

198.   Bickerstaff, Joyce. "Mrs. Roosevelt and Mrs. Bethune: Collaborators
       for Racial Justice." *Social Justice* 48, no.7 (November-December
       1984): 532-535.

       An analysis of the unique and unprecedented friendship between
       Eleanor Roosevelt and Mary McLeod Bethune.

199.   Breen, William J. "Black Women and the Great War: Mobilization
       and Reform in the South." *Journal of Southern History* 44, no.3
       (August 1978): 421-440.

       Discusses the effort to organize southern black women at the
       state level in order to aid the general war effort during the
       First World War. Beside patriotic programs, women's

organizations provided social services to the black community and pushed for increased job opportunities for black women available as a result of the war.

200. Brooks, Evelyn. "The Feminist Theology of the Black Baptist Church, 1880-1900." in *Class, Race, and Sex: The Dynamics of Control*. Edited by Amy Swerdlow and Hanna Lessinger. Boston: G.K. Hall, 1983, pp. 31-59.

Analyzes the progressive views of black women leaders in the Black Baptist Church who advocated an expanded role for women which included work as well as homemaking. These women occupied leadership roles in their church and considered themselves the intellectual equals of men.

201. Bryce, Herrington J., and Alan E. Warrick. "Black Women in Elected Offices." *The Black Scholar* 6, no.2 (October 1974): 17-20.

Says that the number of black women elected to public office has increased about fifty percent between 1969 and 1973, but black women are still underrepresented among all elected officials.

202. Coleman, Willie M. "Keeping the Faith and Disturbing the Peace: Black Women: From Anti-Slavery to Women's Suffrage." Ph.D. diss., University of California, Irvine, 1982.

Covers the history of black women in the anti-slavery and women's suffrage movements. Focuses on the relationship between the two movements and the tension between the struggle against racism and the suppression of women.

203. Davis, Angela Y. *Women, Race and Class*. New York: Random House, 1981.

Essays on the history of black women in the United States in which Davis discusses the historical relationship between the black liberation movement and the women's rights movement. She begins by discussing the position of black women in slavery. She says black men and women were essentially equal partners in the family and in the work they performed. Other topics discussed are the beginning of the women's movement as an offshoot of the anti-slavery movement, racism in the nineteenth-century women's movement, the black women's club movement, and the crusade to end lynching. Although it lacks an introduction, it is a valuable work because it pulls together a great deal of diverse material.

204.   De Graaf, Lawrence B. "Race, Sex, and Region: Black Women in
       the American West, 1850-1920." *Pacific Historical Review* 49,
       no.2 (1980): 285-313.

       Compares the experiences of black women to those of white
       women in the settlement of the American West. Concludes that
       black women did not find greater freedom in the West. They
       were subject to the same denial of basic civil rights, social
       ostracism and segregation as in other areas of the United
       States.

205.   Dickson, Lynda F. "The Early Club Movement Among Black Women
       in Denver: 1890-1925." Ph.D. diss., University of Colorado,
       Boulder, 1982.

       Studied the club movement in Denver as a microcosm of the
       larger national movement among Afro-American women.

206.   Giddings, Paula. *When and Where I Enter: The Impact of Black
       Women on Race and Sex.* New York: William Morrow, 1984.

       A narrative history of black women, tracing their concerns from
       the seventeenth century to the present. Uses the words of
       articulate black women as recorded in their letters and other
       writings to tell their story. Believes that black women were the
       linchpin between the two most important social reform
       movements in American history, the struggle for black rights
       and women's rights.

207.   Gilkes, Cheryl T. "'Together and in Harness:' Women's Traditions
       in the Sanctified Church." *Signs: Journal of Women in Culture
       and Society* 10, no.4 (Summer 1985): 678-699.

       Discusses the role and traditions of women in black Protestant
       churches. Says that in some of these churches black women
       were able to achieve powerful positions of influence and
       structural authority.

208.   Gill, Gerald R . "'Win or Lose-We Win:'the 1952 Vice Presidential
       Campaign of Charlotta A. Bass." in *The Afro-American Woman:
       Struggles and Images.* Edited by Sharon Harley and Rosalyn
       Terborg-Penn. Port Washington, New York: Kennikat Press,
       1978, pp. 109-118.

       Describes the campaign of Charlotta Bass, a civil rights activist
       in California, who ran as the vice-presidential candidate of the
       Progressive party in 1952.

209.   Gregory, Chester W. "Black Women in Pre-Federal America." in
       Clio Was a Woman: Studies in the History of American Women.

Edited by Mabel E. Deutrich and Virginia C. Purdy.
Washington D.C.: Howard University Press, 1980, pp. 53-70.

An overview article surveying the role of free black women and
slave women in eighteenth-century America. Includes a
discussion of the participation of black women in the
Revolutionary War.

210. Hamilton, Tullia K.B. "The National Association of Colored Women,
      1896-1920." Ph.D. diss., Emory University, 1978.

      Examines the history and significance of the work of this
      organization. Profiles characteristics of the leadership of the
      club based upon data from over one hundred former members.
      Asserts that grassroots efforts by women's clubs to secure civil
      rights for blacks was an important factor in the long fight
      against racism in the United States.

211. Harper, Marieta L. "Black Women and the Development of Black
      Politics." *Journal of Afro-American Issues 5*, no.3 (Summer
      1977): 276-284.

      Summarizes the legislative proposals of a small sample of black
      women legislators in the areas of education, civil and women's
      rights, criminal justice, anti-war proposals, and consumer
      protection.

212. Henry, L.J. "Promoting Historical Consciousness: the Early Archives
      Committee of the National Council of Negro Women." *Signs:
      Journal of Women in Culture and Society 7*, no.1 (Autumn 1981):
      251-259.

      Sets forth the efforts of the National Council of Negro Women
      to collect documents promoting historical awareness of the
      accomplishments of black women.

213. Hine, Darlene, and Kate Wittenstein. "Female Slave Resistance: The
      Economics of Sex." in *The Black Woman Cross-Culturally*.
      Edited by Filomina Chioma Steady. Cambridge, Mass.:
      Schenkman Publishing Co., 1981, pp. 289-299.

      Concerned with the ways female slaves resisted the slave system
      through such means as abortion and infanticide.

214. Jenkins, Maude T. "The History of the Black Women's Club
      Movement in America." Ed.D. diss., Columbia University
      Teacher's College, 1984.

Investigates the history of The National Association of Colored
Women in the anti-lynching crusade, prison reform, settlement
house work, and the suffrage movement.

215. Jones, Beverly W. "Mary Church Terrell and the National
      Association of Colored Women, 1896 to 1901." *Journal of Negro
      History* 67 (Spring 1982): 20-33.

      States that the National Association of Colored Women was
      formed to combat discrimination against black women and
      promote racial uplift through various social reform efforts such
      as establishment of kindergartens, nurseries, mother's clubs,
      homes for girls, the aged, and the infirm. Highlights the role
      of Mrs. Terrell, the club's first president, in these endeavors.

216. Jones, Jacqueline. "'My Mother Was Much of a Woman:' Black
      Women, Work, and the Family Under Slavery." *Feminist Studies*
      8, no.2 (Summer 1982): 235-269.

      Asserts that feminist scholarship has neglected the study of
      slave women as a group, and says there is no systematic study
      of the roles of women in slavery. Hence, this article focuses on
      the role of black women in slavery during the years 1830 to
      1860. Jones says that although male and female slaves did
      equivalent work in the fields (except during pregnancy and
      nursing), in their own quarters slaves followed a division of
      labor based on gender which originated in West Africa.

217. Lebsock, Suzanne. "Free Black Women and the Question of
      Matriarchy: Petersburg, Virginia, 1784-1820." *Feminist Studies* 8,
      no.2 (Summer 1982): 271-292.

      See item 218.

218. Lebsock, Suzanne. *The Free Women of Petersburg: Status and
      Culture in a Southern Town.* New York: Norton, 1984.

      A study based on local records for the town of Petersburg,
      Virginia from 1784 to 1860. Lebsock was interested in women's
      attitudes and values and how they might be different from those
      of men. Says that among the free black inhabitants of the
      town, women headed well over half of the households. Most
      free black women were employed as seamstresses or laundresses,
      and they worked because of economic necessity. Black males
      were either not present or not free. Lebsock states that these
      free black women were not matriarchs.

219. Lerner, Gerda. "Black and White Women in Interaction and
      Confrontation." Chap. 7. in *The Majority Finds Its Past:*

Placing Women in History. New York: Oxford University Press, 1979, pp. 94-111.

Traces the interaction of black and white women activists in the anti-slavery, suffrage, women's club and the anti-lynching movements.

220. Lerner, Gerda. "Black Women in the United States: A Problem in Historiography and Interpretation." Chap. 5. in *The Majority Finds Its Past: Placing Women in History.* New York: Oxford University Press, 1979, pp. 63-82.

An overview of the history of black women in the United States focusing on the double oppression experienced by women of color on account of gender as well as race. Says that this oppression originated in slavery in which black women were used as sexual objects by their white masters.

221. Loewenberg, Bert J., and Ruth Bogin, eds. *Black Women in Nineteenth-Century American Life: Their Words, Their Thoughts, Their Feelings.* University Park, Pa.: Pennsylvania State University Press, 1976.

A collection of original source material including letters, memoirs, and interviews with former slaves. The lives of twenty-four women are portrayed here. All of them were born before or during the Civil War. Famous as well as little-known women are included like the former slave who is known only as Cornelia. Makes an excellent addition to reading lists for courses on the history of black women.

222. Neverton-Morton, Cynthia. "The Black Woman's Struggle for Equality in the South, 1895-1925." in *The Afro-American Woman: Struggles and Images.* Edited by Sharon Harley and Rosalyn Terborg-Penn. Port Washington, New York: Kennikat Press, 1978, pp. 5-16.

Describes efforts of various southern black women's groups to organize on the local level to improve black schools and provide other services such as day care centers.

223. Newman, Debra L. "Black Women in the Era of the American Revolution in Pennsylvania." *Journal of Negro History* 61 (July 1976): 276-289.

Describes the lives and occupations of slave and free black women in eighteenth-century Pennsylvania.

224. Noble, Jeanne L. *Beautiful, Also, Are the Souls of My Black Sisters: A History of the Black Woman in America.* Englewood Cliffs, N.J.: Prentice-Hall, 1978.

The title of this book is somewhat deceptive, since it is not strictly a history. The first chapter discusses historical origins in ancient Ethiopia, Egyptian queens, and women warriors. Other sections are concerned with Afro-American women writers from the eighteenth century through the Harlem Renaissance, and black women musicians. Primarily based on secondary sources.

225. Perkins, Linda. "Black Women and Racial 'Uplift' Prior to Emancipation." in *The Black Woman Cross-Culturally.* Edited by Filomina Chioma Steady. Cambridge, Mass.: Schenkman Publishing Co., 1981, pp. 317-333.

Summarizes the self-help activities of black women prior to emancipation. These included forming mutual aid and benevolent societies which pooled members' funds to help each other in time of need, forming abolitionist organizations, and starting schools to educate slaves and former slaves.

226. Sacks, Karen. "Class Roots of Feminism." *Monthly Review* 27, no.9 (February 1976): 28-48.

Traces the class origins of various factions of the nineteenth-century women's movement and labor movement. Points out the racist, anti-worker tendencies of the middle-class suffrage movement.

227. Sealander, Judith A. "Antebellum Black Press Images of Women." *The Western Journal of Black Studies* 6, no.3 (Fall 1982): 159-165.

A study of the image of black women in antebellum black newspapers. Finds that for the most part, articles aimed at black women imitated the idealized image of Victorian women found in the white press.

228. Snorgrass, J. William. "Black Women and Journalism: 1800-1950." *Western Journal of Black Studies* 6, no.3 (Fall 1982): 150-158.

Demonstrates the fact that black women have been an integral part of American journalism from the mid-1800s to the present. Cites the names of many little-known black women journalists, as well as more prominent names such as Ida B. Wells.

229. Sterling, Dorothy, ed. *We Are Your Sisters: Black Women in The 19th Century.* New York: Norton, 1984.

A collection of primary documents portraying the lives of black women between the years 1800 to the 1880s. It includes excerpts from diaries and autobiographies, letters, oral testimonies, and newspaper accounts. Contains sections on slavery, northern free women of color and the abolitionists, the Civil War years, freedwomen in the South, the post-war North, and a special section with excerpts from four diaries. Three of these were written by little-known black women: Frances Rollin, Mary Virginia Montgomery, and Laura Hamilton. An excellent sourcebook of primary materials illustrating the lives and work of black women in the nineteenth century. Recommended for use in women's studies and Afro-American studies courses.

230. Stetson, Erlene. "Black Feminism in Indiana, 1893-1933." *Phylon* 44, no.4 (December 1983): 292-298.

Focuses on the philanthropic activities and achievements of the black women's club movement in Indiana.

231. Sumler-Lewis, Janice. "The Forten-Purvis Women of Philadelphia and the American Anti-Slavery Crusade." *Journal of Negro History* 66 (Winter 1981): 281-288.

Discusses the participation of three generations of black women, the descendants of a wealthy, black Philadelphia freedman, James Forten Sr., in the anti-slavery movement.

232. Terborg-Penn, Rosalyn. "Discrimination Against Afro-American Women in the Woman's Movement, 1830-1920." in *The Black Woman Cross-Culturally*. Edited by Filomina Chioma Steady. Cambridge, Mass.: Schenkman Publishing Co., 1981, pp. 301-314.

Asserts that black women were discriminated against by white women and excluded from participating in the abolitionist, suffrage, temperance and women's club movements. Consequently, black women formed their own organizations to deal with these issues and other race related concerns.

233. Terborg-Penn, Rosalyn. "Nineteenth Century Black Women and Woman Suffrage." *Potomac Review* 7, no.3 (1977): 13-24.

Gives the names and activities of several little-known Afro-American women who were active in the nineteenth-century women's rights movement.

234. Terborg-Penn, Rosalyn. "Teaching the History of Black Women: A Bibliographical Essay." *History Teacher* 13, no.2 (1980): 245-250.

A short essay surveying sources for the study of Afro-American women in United States history. Points out the scarcity of available materials, and provides suggestions for areas where research is needed.

235. White, Deborah G. *Ar'n't I a Woman?: Female Slaves in the Plantation South*. New York: Norton, 1985.

An in-depth study of female slaves in the antebellum South based on interviews with former slaves conducted by the Works Project Administration and firsthand accounts from journals and memoirs. Argues that slave women did not take a subordinate role to that of male slaves and relationships between the sexes were based on mutual respect and equality. Has chapters on the myths of Jezebel and Mammy, the nature of slavery, the female slave life cycle, female slave networks, and family life.

Literature and the Arts

236. Bakerman, Jane S. "Failures of Love: Female Initiation in the Novels of Toni Morrison." *American Literature: A Journal of Literary History, Criticism, and Bibliography* 52, no.4 (January 1981): 541-563.

Provides an in-depth explication of the major female characters in Morrison's *The Bluest Eye*, *Sula*, and *Song of Solomon* centered around the theme of the initiation rite and exploration of adolescent love.

237. Bell, Roseann et al. *Sturdy Black Bridges: Visions of Black Women in Literature*. New York: Doubleday, 1979.

Contains literary criticism as well as a section of short fiction and poetry by American, African, and Caribbean writers. Part II contains interviews with black writers and critics. Aimed at both academic and popular audiences.

238. Bowles, Juliette, ed. *In the Memory and Spirit of Frances, Zora, and Lorraine: Essays and Interviews on Black Women and Writing*. Washington D.C.: Institute for the Arts and the Humanities, Howard University, 1979.

Contains short articles and interviews with Ntozake Shange, Audre Lorde, and Gwendolyn Brooks.

239. Branzberg, Judith V. "Women Novelists of the Harlem Renaissance: A Study in Marginality." Ph.D. diss., University of Massachusetts, 1983.

A study of the novels of Jessie Fauset, Nella Larsen, and Zora Neale Hurston. Maintains the writings of these women contribute to our understanding of the sociological and psychological concept of marginality.

240. Brown, Elizabeth. "Six Female Playwrights: Images of Blacks in Plays by Lorraine Hansberry, Alice Childress, Sonia Sanchez, Barbara Molette, Martie Charles and Ntozake Shange." Ph.D. diss., Florida State University, 1980.

Uses a socio-psychological approach to examine the images of black men and women in the plays of the six playwrights of the title. Concludes that black women dramatists have a different outlook than black male playwrights. Finds that the images of the males in these plays are all negative, whereas the images of the females are mostly positive.

241. Brown, Martha H. "Images of Black Women: Family Roles in Harlem Renaissance Literature." Ph.D. diss., Carnegie-Mellon University, 1976.

An analysis of the attitudes towards black women as grandmothers, mothers, mates, and daughters in works of male and female writers of the Harlem Renaissance.

242. Burke, Virginia M. "Zora Neale Hurston and Fannie Hurst as They Saw Each Other." *College Language Association Journal* 20, no.4 (June 1977): 435-447.

An unusual article which juxtaposes the life and work of Zora Neale Hurston with the life and career of Fannie Hurst. Hurston was employed briefly in the 1920s by Hurst as a secretary. Says that Hurston understood Hurst better than Hurst understood Hurston.

243. Burwell, Sherri L. "The Soul of Black Women: The Hermeneutical Method of Analysis as Applied to the Novel *Corregidora*." Ph.D. diss., California School of Professional Psychology, 1979.

Uses African philosophy and Jungian theory to analyze the novel *Corregidora* by Gayle Jones in an attempt to better understand the lives of contemporary women of color.

244. Byerman, Keith E. "Intense Behaviors: The Use of the Grotesque in *The Bluest Eye* and *Eva's Man*." *College Language Association Journal* 25 (June 1982): 447-457.

Says that the grotesque action such as the incest in Morrison's *The Bluest Eye* and the necrophilia and castration in Gayle Jones' *Eva's Man* represent vehicles for criticizing America's treatment of blacks and women.

245.   Cannon, Katie G. "Resources for a Constructive Ethic for Black
        Women with Special Attention to the Life and Work of Zora
        Neale Hurston." Ph.D. diss., Union Theological Seminary in the
        City of New York, 1983.

        Examines the literary tradition of black women authors focusing
        on the life and work of Zora Hurston. Says that Afro-American
        women developed distinctive moral characteristics such as the
        ability to survive racial, gender, and class oppression, and this
        is reflected in the literature of women of color. Hurston's life
        and work exemplifies this tradition.

246.   Christian, Barbara. *Black Feminist Criticism: Perspectives on Black
        Women Writers*. New York: Pergamon, 1985.

        A collection of previously published essays discussing the novels
        and short fiction of Alice Walker, Toni Morrison, Paule
        Marshall, Gwendolyn Brooks, and Ntozaka Shange. Concerned
        with some current themes in black women's literature such as
        lesbianism and black feminism. Each essay is preceded with a
        brief introductory note by the author explaining the background
        for the article.

247.   Christian, Barbara. *Black Women Novelists: The Development of a
        Tradition, 1892-1976*. Westport, Conn.: Greenwood Press, 1980.
        An examination of the black woman as novelist. The first three
        chapters discuss the development of fiction by black women
        writers during the period 1860 to 1960. The following three
        chapters are devoted to three authors: Paule Marshall, Toni
        Morrison, and Alice Walker. The final chapter summarizes the
        tradition of black women as writers of fiction.

248.   Cliff, Michelle. "'I Found God In Myself and I Loved Her Fiercely';
        More Thoughts on the Work of Black Women Artists." in
        *Women, Feminist Identity and Society in the 1980'S: Selected
        Papers*. Edited by Myriam Diaz-Diocaretz and Iris M. Zavela.
        Philadelphia: Benjamins Publishing Co., 1985, pp. 101-126.

        Explores the connection between the art and music of Afro-
        American women and the art forms and mythology of their
        African ancestors. Illustrates her thesis by describing the
        symbolism in a quilt made by the daughter of African slaves.

249.   Cliff, Michelle. "Object to Subject: Some Thoughts on the Work of
        Black Women Artists." *Heresies* 4, no.3 (1982): 34-38.

        Critically examines the works of four Afro-American women
        artists: the sculptor, Edmonia Lewis (1843-1900?), the
        contemporary artist, Elizabeth Catlett, the nineteenth-century

quilt-maker, Harriet Powers (1837-1911), and the modern artist, Betye Saar.

250. Dandridge, Rita B. "Male Critics/Black Women's Novels." *College Language Association Journal* 23 (September 1979): 1-11.

Asserts that male critics, both black and white, have not fairly evaluated writings of American black women. Says these critics can be categorized as either apathetic, chauvinistic, or paternalistic in their approach to literature by Afro-American women authors.

251. Dearborn, Mary V. "Black Women Authors and the Harlem Renaissance." Chap. 3. in *Pocahontas's Daughters: Gender and Ethnicity in American Culture*. New York: Oxford University Press, 1986, pp. 48-70.

Discusses the work of Jessie Fauset, Nella Larsen, and Zora Neale Hurston. Sees Fauset as a mediator between black culture and white culture in that she tries to bring the two together by asserting their sameness. Says that Larsen is an example of the ethnic woman caught between two worlds and her heroines do not feel wholly a part of the black or the white world. Declares that Zora Hurston overcame difficulties and controversies to produce *Their Eyes Were Watching God*, a brilliant novel of female independence.

252. Dearborn, Mary V. "Miscegenation and the Mulatto, Inheritance and Incest: The Pocahontas Marriage, Part II." Chap 6. in *Pocahontas's Daughters: Gender and Ethnicity in America*. New York: Oxford University Press, 1986, pp. 131-158.

Analyzes the themes of miscegenation and the tragic mulatto in the writings of black women novelists from Frances Harper's *Iola Leroy* to Gayle Jones' 1975 novel *Corregidora* as part of a broader theme of gender and ethnicity in American literature.

253. Denniston, Dorothy L. "Cultural Reclamation: The Development of a Pan-African Sensibility in the Fiction of Paule Marshall." Ph.D. diss., Brown University, 1983.

A study of the artistic development of Paule Marshall. Contends that over time Marshall developed a Pan-African sensibility in her works.

254. Diaz-Diocaretz, Myriam. "Black North American Women Poets in the Semeiotics of Culture." in *Women, Feminist Identity, and Society in the 1980'S: Selected Papers*. Edited by Myriam Diaz-Diocaretz and Iris M. Zavela. Philadelphia: Benjamins Publishing Co., 1985, pp. 37-60.

Asserts that the poetry of contemporary North American black women is translinguistic and transcultural because it uses Black English as well as standard English, and it refers to Africa in addition to American black culture.

255. Evans, Mari, ed. *Black Women Writers, 1950-1980*. New York: Doubleday, 1984.

A compilation of literary criticism of fifteen American black women authors. All of the contributions were specially commissioned for this book. Statements by the authors on the nature of their own work are included. Authors discussed are: Maya Angelou, Toni Cade Bambara, Gwendolyn Brooks, Alice Childress, Lucille Clifton, Mari Evans, Nikki Giovanni, Gayle Jones, Audre Lorde, Paule Marshall, Toni Morrison, Carolyn Rodgers, Soni Sanchez, Alice Walker, and Margaret Walker. Bio/bibliographical information is included for some of the authors.

256. Fisher, Jerilyn B. "The Minority Woman's Voice: A Cultural Study of Black and Chicano Fiction." Ph.D. diss., The American University, 1978.

Deals with contemporary women writers of both black and Chicano fiction. Writers studied are Toni Morrison, Alice Walker, and Estela Portillo. Uses sociological research to support literary interpretations.

257. *Forever Free: Art by African American Women, 1862-1980*. Alexandria, Virginia: Stephenson, 1980.

An exhibition catalog containing biographical sketches of each of the forty-nine artists whose work is included in this exhibition.

258. Foster, Frances S. "Octavia Butler's Black Female Future Fiction." *Extrapolation* 23, no.1 (Spring 1982): 37-49.

Discusses how Butler's science fiction novels explore the impact of race and sex upon future society.

259. Govan, Sandra Y. "Gwendolyn Bennett: Portrait of an Artist Lost." Ph.D. diss., Emory University, 1980.

Uses oral history to research the life of this little-known black woman artist who was active during the Harlem Renaissance.

260. Green, Mildred D. *Black Women Composers: A Genesis*. Boston: Twayne Publishers, 1983.

Examines the works of five twentieth-century black women composers of jazz, blues, and spirituals: Florence Price, Margaret Bonds, Julia Perry, Evelyn Pittmen, and Lena McLin. Surveys the life and career of each of the above composers.

261. Gwin, Minrose C. *Black and White Women of the Old South: The Peculiar Sisterhood in American Literature.* Knoxville, Tenn.: University of Tennessee Press, 1985.

Studies the relationship between women of color and white women in fictional portrayals of the Antebellum, Civil War, and Reconstruction South. Works examined are *Uncle Tom's Cabin, Absalom, Absalom!* and Margaret Walker's *Jubilee*. Gwin's general conclusion is that black women are not regarded as individuals by white women in fictional works by white authors, but are seen in terms of stereotypes such as child-like creatures or as servants.

262. Handy, D. Antoinette. *Black Women in American Bands and Orchestras.* Metuchen, N.J.: Scarecrow Press, 1981.

A survey of black women in American bands and orchestras arranged by the type of instrument played. Also has some short profiles of individual instrumentalists.

263. Handy, D. Antoinette. *The International Sweethearts of Rhythm.* Metuchen, N.J.: Scarecrow Press, 1983.

A history of an all-woman jazz band which was on a par with other dance bands in the 1940s. Based on recollections of the performers. Contains numerous photographs.

264. Harris, Trudier. *Black Women in the Fiction of James Baldwin.* Knoxville, Tenn.: University of Tennessee Press, 1985.

Critically examines the female characters in the novels and short stories of James Baldwin. Classifies most of these characters as playing traditional feminine roles as wives, sisters, church-goers, or fallen women. Sees most of Baldwin's characters as guilt-ridden, and believes that none of his women characters are as equally important as his male characters.

265. Harris, Trudier. *From Mammies to Militants: Domestics in Black American Literature.* Philadelphia: Temple University Press, 1982.

Analyzes eleven works of fiction in which domestics appear as central characters. The stories examined are set in both the North and the South and were written between the early 1900's to 1970. The author's purpose is to determine if the characters are stereotyped or presented as three-dimensional. Identifies three stages of progression portrayed in the literature: 1. the mammy or typical southern maid. 2. the transitional or moderate figures who hide their true personality behind a compliant mask. 3. the militants.

266.   Harris, Trudier. "Three Black Women Writers and Humanism: A Folk Perspective." in *Black American Literature and Humanism*. Edited by R. Baxter Miller. Lexington, Kentucky: University Press of Kentucky, 1981, pp. 50-74.

Examines works by Sarah E. Wright, Alice Walker, and Paule Marshall.

267.   Harrison, Daphne D. "Black Women in the Blues Tradition." in *The Afro-American Woman: Struggles and Images*. Edited by Sharon Harley and Rosalyn Terborg-Penn. Port Washington, N.Y.: Kennikat Press, 1978, pp. 58-73.

Surveys a wide range of black women who were performers in the Classic Blues Era (1920-1933). Says poverty influenced the careers of many of these performers, and the unique lyrics of their songs reflect the harsh realities of the oppressive societal conditions in which they lived.

268.   Hemenway, Robert E. *Zora Neale Hurston: A Literary Biography*. Urbana, Illinois: University of Illinois Press, 1977.

A carefully researched work which seeks to clarify the life of the writer and folklorist. When work on this book began, very little accurate information on Hurston was available in print. Hemenway's book rescues Hurston from almost complete obscurity. Frequently cited as the authoritative account of Hurston's life.

269.   Henderson, Mae G. "*The Color Purple*: Revisions and Redefinitions." *Sage: A Scholarly Journal on Black Women* 2, no.1 (Spring 1985): 14-18.

Says that Walker takes a traditionally European, male-controlled form, the epistolary novel, and transforms it into a novel of female bonding.

270.   Holloway, Karla F.C. "A Critical Investigation of Literary and Linguistic Structures in the Fiction of Zora Neale Hurston." Ph.D. diss., Michigan State University, 1978.

Investigates from two perspectives, literary and linguistic, the use of black dialect in Hurston's fiction. Especially interested in her use of the narrative voice.

271. Holt, Elvin. "Zora Neale Hurston and the Politics of Race: A Study of Selected Nonfictional Works." Ph.D. diss., University of Kentucky, 1983.

Examines Hurston's nonfiction including *Tell My Horse* and *Dust Tracks on a Road*, as well as, selected essays, book reviews, and newspaper articles to uncover her views on the politics of race.

272. Howard, Lillie P. "Nanny and Janie: Will the Twain Ever Meet? (A Look at Zora Neale Hurston's *Their Eyes Were Watching God*)." *Journal of Black Studies* 12 (June 1982): 404-414.

Concerned with explicating Janie's search for self-fulfillment in Hurston's *Their Eyes Were Watching God*.

273. Howard, Lillie P. *Zora Neale Hurston*. Boston: Twayne Publishers, 1980.

A critical analysis of the life and writings of Hurston. The first chapter covers her life and times. Chapters 2 and 3 discuss her short fiction. Additional chapters are devoted to each of her four novels, and the last chapter talks about her works of nonfiction. Based on the author's dissertation.

274. Hull, Gloria T. "Black Women Poets from Wheatley To Walker." *Negro American Literature Forum* 9 (1975): 91-96.

Surveys black women as poets from the eighteenth century to 1945. Says the earlier poets are often overlooked because of the explosion of black women poets in the contemporary period.

275. Hull, Gloria T. *Color, Sex, and Poetry: Three Women of the Harlem Renaissance*. Bloomington, Indiana: Indiana University Press, 1987.

A literary and biographical study of three neglected female poets of the Harlem Renaissance: Alice Dunbar-Nelson, Angelina Weld Grimke, and Georgia Douglas Johnson. Hull bases her reassessment of these writers on hitherto unknown biographical and critical material about them, which she says corrects the myopic view of them as women and as writers. Considers them to be elder stateswomen and literary foremothers for the generation of writers which succeeded them.

276. Hull, Gloria T. "Rewriting Afro-American Literature: A Case for Black Women Writers." *The Radical Teacher* 6 (April 1978): 10-13.

Urges teachers to include literature by black women in Afro-
American and Women's Studies courses. Asserts that black
women have been left out of the Afro-American literary canon.

277. Hull, Gloria T. "'Under the days': The Buried Life and Poetry of
      Angelina Weld Grimke." *Conditions Five* 2, no.2 (Autumn 1979):
      17-25.

      Concludes that this little-known poet of the early twentieth
      century lived a sad, buried life because of her thwarted
      lesbianism.

278. Hurston, Zora Neale. *Dust Tracks on a Road: An Autobiography.*
      2d ed., edited by Robert E. Hemenway. Urbana, Illinois:
      University of Illinois, 1984.

      This new edition of the 1942 work contains three chapters
      which were edited out of the original manuscript because they
      contained inflammatory, anti-American remarks. Includes an
      informative introduction by Robert E. Hemenway which pro-
      vides background information about Hurston and her
      autobiography.

279. Ingram, Elwanda D. "Black Women: Literary Self-Portraits." Ph.D.
      diss., University of Oregon, 1980.

      Studies female literary characters in a full range of black
      literature by male and female authors. Places these characters
      into four main types: suspended, color-conscious, assimilated, and
      emergent-assertive. Argues that black women writers have
      created characters that are full-dimensional.

280. Isani, Mukhtar A. "The British Reception of Wheatley's *Poems on
      Various Subjects.*" *Journal of Negro History* 66 (Summer 1981):
      144-149.

      Consists of excerpts from nine original reviews of Wheatley's
      collection of poetry published in London in 1773. All of the
      reviews were favorable and viewed her writing as a remarkable
      achievement considering the fact that she had no formal
      education.

281. Issacs, Diane S. "Ann Petry's Life and Art: Piercing Stereotypes."
      Ph.D. diss., Columbia University, 1982.

      Aims to offer a "comprehensive, critical study of Ann Petry's
      life and art." The first three chapters cover the writer's life
      and career. The last three chapters are devoted to a critical
      examination of Petry's major works.

282. Jackson, Irene V. "Black Women and Music: A Survey from Africa to the New World." *Minority Voices: An Interdisciplinary Journal of Literature and the Arts* 2, no.2 (1979): 15-27.

Investigates the relationship between the music of Africa and the New World. Says that African women were the main participants in musical rituals held at rites of passage such as puberty, marriage, childbirth, and funerals. This tradition was continued in the New World with spirituals and lullabies sung by slave women and by the blues singers of the 1920s and 1930s.

283. Jenkins, Joyce O. "To Make a Woman Black: A Critical Analysis of the Women Characters in the Fiction and Folklore of Zora Neale Hurston." Ph.D. diss., Bowling Green State University, 1978.

Asserts that Hurston's female characters are well-drawn. Looks at three predominant themes in her writings: love, religion, and race in relationship to her characters.

284. Johnson, Gloria J. "Hurston's Folk: The Critical Significance of Afro-American Folk Tradition in the Three Novels and the Autobiography." Ph.D. diss., University of California at Irvine, 1978.

A study of the relationship between Hurston's folk characters and their prototypes in black folklore. Aims to establish folklore as a valid method of evaluating literature.

285. Keizs, Marcia V. "The Development of a Dialectic: Private and Public Patterns in the Work of Margaret Walker and Gwendolyn Brooks." Ed.D. diss., Columbia University Teachers College, 1984.

Identifies two impulses in the work and careers of these authors which are labeled public and private. Says that private, domestic concerns roughly match a feminine focus, whereas works which center on political and social concerns roughly matches a masculine orientation. Concludes with a summary of the contribution of Brooks and Walker to the tradition of black women's literature.

286. Koolish, Lynda L. "A Whole New Poetry Beginning Here: Contemporary American Women Poets." Ph.D. diss., Stanford University, 1981.

An analysis of contemporary feminist poetry. Chapter 3 is on women of color with Audre Lorde's poetry a central focus. Discusses the themes of racism in the women's movement and the intersection of racism and sexism.

287.   Lee, Valerie G. "The Use of Folktalk in Novels by Black Women
       Writers." *College Language Association Journal* 23, no.3 (March
       1980): 266-272.

       Discusses the use of folk language in portraying the relationship
       between the sexes in three novels by black women authors:
       Their Eyes Were Watching God, Sula, and *Corregidora.*

288.   Lewis, Vashti C. "The Mulatto Woman as Major Character in
       Novels by Black Women, 1892-1937." Ph.D. diss., University of
       Iowa, 1981.

       Surveys the major female characters in thirteen novels by black
       women novelists written during the period 1892 to 1937.
       Authors whose works are examined include Frances E.W. Harper,
       Pauline Hopkins, Jessie Fauset, Nella Larsen, and Zora Neale
       Hurston. Lewis compares the fictional characters with historical
       images of black women during the period in which the novels
       were set. Concludes that Hurston was the first of the writers
       examined here to depict characters historically representative of
       southern, rural black women.

289.   Lieb, Sandra R. *Mother of the Blues: A Study of Ma Rainey.*
       Amherst, Mass.: University of Massachusetts Press, 1981.

       A comprehensive study which argues that Gertrude (Ma) Rainey
       laid the foundation on which other classic blues performers such
       as Bessie Smith enlarged upon. Includes an overview of her
       life, a discussion of her performance style, and an analysis of
       the themes of her recorded songs.

290.   Lynch, Charles H. "Robert Hayden and Gwendolyn Brooks: A
       Critical Study." Ph.D. diss., New York University, 1977.

       Compares the work of Hayden and Brooks using evaluation and
       analysis to discuss why they "cannot be neatly categorized as
       racial apologists, propagandists, or spokespersons." Examines
       their lives, their history of publication, criticism, literary
       influences, quality of their poetry and the milieu in which they
       wrote.

291.   McCredie, Wendy J. "Authority and Authorization in *Their Eyes
       Were Watching God.*" *Black American Literature Forum* 16
       (Spring 1982): 25-28.

       Examines Janie's relationships with her grandmother and the men
       in her life in Hurston's novel in order to analyze Janie's search
       for autonomy and selfhood.

292. McDowell, Deborah E. "New Directions for Black Feminist Criticism." *Black American Literature Forum* 14, no.4 (Winter 1980): 153-158.

    Acknowledges that black women writers have been ignored, misunderstood, and summarily dismissed by white women scholars and black male scholars alike. However, McDowell is critical of black feminist scholarship to date, particularly Barbara Smith's article on black feminist criticism. (See item 323.) She believes it has been marred by slogans, rhetoric, and idealism, and has oversimplified the issue of lesbianism. She says there is a need for a sound, thorough articulation of the black feminist aesthetic.

293. McDowell, Deborah E. "Women on Women: The Black Woman Writer of the Harlem Renaissance." Ph.D. diss., Purdue University, 1979.

    A feminist reading of the novels of Jessie Fauset, Nella Larsen, and Zora Neale Hurston. Examines the psychology of the black female character in the works of these authors.

294. McKay, Nellie. "An Interview With Toni Morrison." *Contemporary Literature* 24, no. 4 (Winter 1983): 413–429.

    Morrison talks about how she creates the characters in her novels; what motivates them, and how they relate to contemporary black life.

295. Malone, Gloria S. "The Nature and Causes of Suffering in the Fiction of Paule Marshall, Kristin Hunter, Toni Morrison, and Alice Walker." Ph.D. diss., Kent State University, 1979.

    Malone finds that suffering is a common theme in the fiction of the four contemporary black authors examined in this study.

296. Martin, Odette E. "Curriculum and Response: A Study of the Images of the Black Woman in Black Fiction." Ph.D. diss., University of Chicago, 1980.

    Outlines methods for teaching a course on black women characters. Examines literary stereotypes and analyzes characters in writings of Nella Larsen, Cyrus Coulter, Alice Walker, and Toni Morrison among others. Provides suggestions for use of methods and materials for classroom use.

297. Melhelm, D.H. "Gwendolyn Brooks: Prophecy and Poetic Process." Ph.D. diss., City University of New York, 1976.

Critically analyzes and places in historical and literary contexts
the poetry of Gwendolyn Brooks. Asserts that Brooks is a
major poet of the twentieth century. Says her work employs a
new, heroic genre which combines elements of Anglo-Saxon and
Greek heroic poetry with elements of black culture such as
syncopation and chanted sermon.

298.   Miller, Jeanne-Marie A. "Angelina Weld Grimke: Playwright and
       Poet." *College Language Association Journal* 21 (June 1978):
       513-524.

       Places Grimke's writing in the tradition of the Black Genteel
       School which tried to depict the positive and progressive aspects
       of black life.

299.   Miller, Jeanne-Marie A. "Images of Black Women in Plays by Black
       Playwrights." *College Language Association Journal* 20 (June
       1977): 494-507.

       Surveys a wide range of female characters in plays by black
       male and female playwrights including Alice Childress, Lorraine
       Hansberry, J.E. Franklin, LeRoi Jones, and Adrienne Kennedy.
       Says the images portrayed are positive for the most part.

300.   Moore, Maxine F. "Characters in the Works of Gwendolyn Brooks."
       Ph.D. diss., Emory University, 1983.

       Looks at changes over time in three groups of characters (men,
       women, and children) in the poetry of Gwendolyn Brooks.
       Examines the impact of Brooks' evolving political views on the
       portrayal of her characters. Says her female characters are the
       least adversely affected by these changes.

301.   Moutoussamy-Ashe, Jeanne. *Viewfinders: Black Women
       Photographers, 1839-1985.* New York: Dodd, Meade and
       Company, 1986.

       Focuses on pioneer black women photographers who have largely
       been lost to history. Divided into five chronological time
       periods, containing biographical sketches and representative
       works of each photographer including many self-portraits.

302.   O'Banner, Bessie M. "A Study of Black Heroines in Four Selected
       Novels (1929-1959) by Four Black American Novelists: Zora Neale
       Hurston, Nella Larsen, Paule Marshall, Ann Lane Petry." Ph.D.
       diss., Southern Illinois University at Carbondale, 1981.

       Looks at the development of female characters in the novels of
       the above four writers. Is primarily concerned with how the

heroines of these novels reconcile the two worlds of black people and white people.

303. Ogunyemi, Chikwenye O. "Womanism: The Dynamics of the Contemporary Black Female Novel in English." *Signs: Journal of Women in Culture and Society* 11, no.1 (Autumn 1985): 63-80.

Distinguishes a black womanist aesthetic among black female novelists in Africa and the United States which is separate from white feminism in that besides dealing with gender issues it also incorporates racial, cultural, national, economic and political considerations.

304. O'Neale, Sondra. "Speaking For Ourselves: Black Women Writers of the 80's." *Southern Exposure* 9, no.2 (1981): 16-19.

Decries the lack of fully developed black women characters in American fiction. Looks at type cast images of Afro-American women such as the Aunt Jemima image, the tragic mulatto and the Jezebel types in literature. Asserts that even black male writers have not been able to portray black women as complex human beings.

305. Oshana, Maryann. *Women of Color: A Filmography of Minority and Third World Women*. New York: Garland, 1985.

Listed here are English-language films which include women of color as major characters. Covers the period 1930 to 1983. Includes brief plot synopses.

306. Pryse, Marjorie, and Hortense J. Spillers, eds. *Conjuring: Black Women, Fiction, and Literary Tradition*. Bloomington, Indiana: Indiana University Press, 1985.

A collection of literary criticism grouped around the theme of black women novelists as conjure women or mediums who, like Alice Walker, recognize their common literary ancestors as gardeners, quilt makers, grandmothers, rootworkers, and women who wrote autobiographies. Examines the literary tradition based on storytelling and magic/folklore. The first two essays look at nineteenth-century autobiographies and slave narratives. Other essays in the collection discuss individual writers: Pauline Hopkins, Jessie Redmon Fauset, Ann Petry, Margaret Walker, Paule Marshall, Toni Morrison, Octavia Butler, and Toni Cade Bambara.

307. Pyne-Timothy, Helen. "Perceptions of the Black Woman in the Work of Claude McKay." *College Language Association Journal* 19, no.2 (December 1975): 152-164.

Says that Claude McKay (1889-1948) portrayed his female characters with great sensitivity and they emerge as multi-faceted creatures. Not a very convincing argument since most of the female characters the author describes appear to be victims.

308. Rich, Adrienne. "The Problem With Lorraine Hansberry." *Freedomways* 19, no.4 (1979): 247-255.

    Reviews the life and work of Hansberry from a white feminist perspective. Asserts that her unpublished writings and the depiction of the women in her plays indicate that Hansberry was a feminist. Suggests she could not openly express her views on the Broadway stage or the television screen in the 1950s and early 1960s and still hope to have her work produced.

309. Rigsby, Gregory. "Phillis Wheatley's Craft as Reflected in Her Revised Elegies." *Journal of Negro Education* 47 (Fall 1978): 402-413.

    Says that Wheatley was a careful craftsperson which is demonstrated with a word-by-word and line-by-line analysis of her elegies.

310. Robinson, William H. *Critical Essays on Phillis Wheatley*. Boston: G.K. Hall, 1982.

    A collection of the commentaries and criticisms of the works of Wheatley arranged chronologically so as to show the evolution of the interpretation of her work.

311. Robinson, William H. *Phillis Wheatley: A Bio-Bibliography*. New York: G.K. Hall, 1981.

    An annotated bibliography arranged chronologically from 1761 until 1979 of the most typical treatments of Phillis Wheatley's life and writings. Includes anthologies, biographies, book reviews, histories, introductions to books, newspapers, magazines, published and manuscript letters, dictionaries, encyclopedias, journals, and books.

312. Robinson, William H. *Phillis Wheatley and Her Writings*. New York: Garland, 1984.

    A listing of the complete collection of the poetry and other writings of Wheatley. Only the several dozen missing poems are not included here.

313. Robinson, William H. *Phillis Wheatley in the Black American Beginnings*. Detroit, Mich.: Broadside Press, 1975.

Attempts to show Wheatley "as someone different from what tradition contends." Organizes and brings up-to-date, research on Wheatley and her writings.

314. Royster, Beatrice H. "The Ironic Vision of Four Black Women Novelists: A Study of the Novels of Jessie Fauset, Nella Larsen, Zora Neale Hurston, and Ann Petry." Ph.D. diss., Emory University, 1975.

Analyzes separately the works of the above four authors. Says they all have in common a sense of irony and alienation.

315. Rushing, Andrea B. "Annotated Bibliography of Images of Black Women in Black Literature." *College Language Association Journal* 21 (March 1978): 435-442.

Lists books and periodical articles published between 1959 to 1977 and provides evaluative comments.

316. Rushing, Andrea B. "Images of Black Women in Afro-American Poetry." in *The Afro-American Woman: Struggles and Images.* Edited by Sharon Harley and Rosalyn Terborg-Penn. Port Washington, N.Y.: Kennikat Press, 1978, pp. 74-84.

Discusses the most common images of black women found in the poetry of black writers. Finds no examples of black women depicted as tragic mulattoes or castrating Sapphires in formal Afro-American poetry. States that for the most part, black women are portrayed as heroic or symbolic in black poetry. Says there is a need for black poetry to reflect the realities of black women's lives.

317. Sadoff, Dianne F. "Matrilineage: The Case of Alice Walker and Zora Neale Hurston." *Signs: Journal of Women in Culture and Society* 11, no.1 (Autumn 1985): 4-26.

Examines Alice Walker's relationship as a writer to her literary precursor, Zora Neale Hurston. Says Walker idealizes Hurston as a model for her own fiction and, in so doing, misreads Hurston.

318. Schmidt, Rita T. "With My Sword in My Hand: The Politics of Race and Sex in the Fiction of Zora Neale Hurston." Ph.D. diss., University of Pittsburgh, 1983.

A feminist reading of Hurston's fiction. Asserts male/female power relations constitute the core of Hurston's narratives, and this aspect of her work has not been addressed thoroughly and comprehensively. Examines factors of race, class, and gender on Hurston's literary self-expression.

319. Schreiber, Sheila O. "Art and Life: The Novels of Black Women."
      Ph.D. diss., University of New Mexico, 1982.

      Uses novels of black female authors to study sociological aspects
      of the lives of women of color in America. Investigates
      thematic similarities in the literature with regard to current
      sociological concerns such as black women's self-concept,
      familial role and the like.

320. Shaw, Harry B. *Gwendolyn Brooks*. Boston: Twayne, 1980.

      Looks at the major themes (death, the labyrinth, and survival)
      in the poetry of Brooks in relationship to the black experience
      in America. In the last chapter Shaw examines Brooks' only
      novel, *Maud Martha*.

321. Shields, John C. "Phillis Wheatley's Poetics of Ascent." Ph.D.
      diss., University of Tennessee, 1978.

      Argues that Wheatley's poetry deserves closer attention then it
      has received in the past. Shields' believes that Wheatley was
      not a derivative imitator of Alexander Pope. His investigation
      reveals that Wheatley was a serious poet and that she is
      deserving of the dignity of aesthetic appreciation.

322. Shockley, Ann A. "The Black Lesbian in American Literature: A
      Critical Overview." *Conditions Five* 2, no.2 (Autumn 1979):
      133-142.

      Reviews some of the recent work by black lesbian writers and
      says that until the last few years there has been almost nothing
      published by black lesbians.

323. Smith, Barbara. "Toward a Black Feminist Criticism." *Women's
      Studies International Quarterly* 2, no.2 (1979): 183-194.

      A ground-breaking essay which argues the need for serious
      consideration of the literature of American black women authors.
      Declares that there is a particular need for a black feminist
      criticism which takes into account the interlocking factors of
      race, sex, and class oppression manifest in the works of women
      of color. Chastises black women critics for not using a
      consistent feminist analysis and not writing about black lesbian
      literature.

324. Spillers, Hortense J. "A Hateful Passion, A Lost Love." *Feminist
      Studies* 9, no.2 (Summer 1983): 293-323.

      Demonstrates changes in black female charactization over time
      from Zora Neale Hurston's Janie in *Their Eyes Were Watching*

God to Margaret Walker's *Jubilee* and Toni Morrison's *Sula*.
States that Walker's Vyry represents a corporate ideal, the black
woman who exists for the race. Hurston's Janie is a more
complex character than Vyry but she is not as complex or
perplexing as the female characters in Morrison's *Sula*. Spiller's
says that Sula lives for herself and she does not serve as a
symbol for the black race as does Vyry. This is an excellent,
complete interpretation of the major characters in the three
novels discussed here.

325. Stanback, Marsha H. "Code-Switching in Black Women's Speech."
Ph.D. diss., University of Massachusetts, 1983.

Compares speech patterns of black females to white females and
black males. Focuses on variable use of Black English
vernacular and mainstream American English dialects by women
speakers in response to different situations. Subjects were
middle-class and college-educated. Concludes that black
participants code-switched between Black English and
Mainstream English, and they varied some Black English features
according to their conversational partners' race or gender.

326. Stockard, Janice L. "The Role of the American Black Woman in
Folktales: An Interdisciplinary Study of Identification and
Interpretation." Ph.D. diss., Tulane University, 1980.

An interdisciplinary study of folktales that contain black women
as main characters. Studied sixty-one American folktales.
Concludes that black females are as well-developed as male
characters in Afro-American folklore.

327. Sylvander, Carolyn W. "Jessie Redmon Fauset, Black American
Writer: Her Relationships, Biographical and Literary, With Black
and White Writers, 1919-1935." Ph.D. diss., University of
Wisconsin at Madison, 1976.

Believes that Fauset has not been fairly or completely studied
by critics and historians of black literature. This study
attempts to remedy the situation.

328. Tate, Claudia, ed. *Black Women Writers at Work*. New York:
Continuum, 1983.

Contains interviews with fourteen black women writers including
Maya Angelou, Gwendolyn Brooks, Nikki Giovanni, Ntozake
Shange, and Alice Walker. Writers comment on their work and
how it has been influenced by their personal lives.

329.   Taylor-Gutherie, Danille. "'And She Was Loved!' The Novels of
       Toni Morrison, A Black Woman's World View." Ph.D. diss.,
       Brown University, 1984.

       Analyzes the works of Morrison in order to illuminate the
       cultural experience of women of color in the United States.
       Employs an interdisciplinary methodology, using elements of
       anthropology, sociology, history, and literature. Contains
       separate chapters on each of Morrison's four novels.

330.   Tener, Robert L. "Adrienne Kennedy's Portrait of the Black
       Woman." *Studies in Black English* 6, no.2 (1975): 1-5.

       An explication of the surrealistic play, *The Owl Answers* by
       Adrienne Kennedy. Says this play is intended to represent the
       fragmented identity of a mulatto woman.

331.   Turner, S.H. Regina. "Images of Black Women in the Plays of Black
       Female Playwrights, 1950-1975." Ph.D. diss., Bowling Green State
       University, 1982.

       Examines the images of Afro-American female characters in
       twenty-eight plays by nine black women playwrights: Childress,
       Hansberry, Jones, Anderson, Sanchez, Kennedy, Charles, Clark-
       Pendarvis, and Stockard Martin. In addition, compares images in
       these plays to those which appeared in the social science
       literature at the time the play was written. Many of the same
       images which appeared in the social science literature appeared
       in the plays as well. Turner observes that racism and sexism
       are seen by black female playwrights as major factors affecting
       the lives of women of color.

332.   Udosen, Willye B. "Image of Black Women in Black American
       Drama, 1900 to 1970." Ed.D. diss., East Texas State University,
       1979.

       Examines the portrayal of Afro-American women in each of the
       seven decades of this study. Sees two types of women
       portrayed: 1. the stereotype and 2. the realistic figure. Says
       that stereotyping is used less frequently in Broadway plays after
       the 1930s.

333.   Varga-Coley, Barbara J. "The Novels of Black American Women."
       Ph.D. diss., State University of New York at Stony Brook, 1980.

       Chronologically looks at the novels of Jessie Fauset, Nella
       Larsen, Zora Neale Hurston, Dorothy West, Ann Petry,
       Gwendolyn Brooks, Kristin Hunter, and Margaret Walker.
       Subjects covered include the significance of color in the
       literature of Afro-American women, the black woman domestic

as a theme, friendship (including interracial friendship) between female characters, and black female stereotypes such as the Mammy.

334. Wade-Gayles, Gloria. *No Crystal Stair: Visions of Race and Sex in Black Women's Fiction.* New York: Pilgrim Press, 1984.

Uses history and sociology to analyze visions of black women in twelve selected novels by black women authors written between 1946 and 1976. Examines how the lives of fictional characters reflect the black woman's struggle to overcome the double jeopardy of racial and sexual oppression in the United States. The first chapter is an historical overview of Afro-American women in America from 1946 to 1976. Chapter 2 compares images of American black women in the media and scholarship with fictional images portrayed in black women's novels. Chapters 3-5 look at specific themes in the novels studied here: marriage and motherhood, black women and hopelessness, and challenges and contradictions. Chapter 6 considers the emerging sexual consciousness of black women as reflected in Alice Walker's character, Meridian and Toni Morrison's Sula.

335. Walker, Alice. *In Search of Our Mothers' Gardens: Womanist Prose.* New York: Harcourt Brace Jovanovich, 1983.

A collection of Walker's essays, articles, presentations, and reviews first written between 1966 and 1982 in which she discusses personal experiences which have influenced her writings. The title of this collection is taken from an essay in it, in which she reflects on the creativity of past generations of women like her own mother who expressed her creativity in the only way she was able, through growing magnificent gardens.

336. Ward, Hazel M. "The Black Woman as Character: Images in the American Novel, 1852-1953." Ph.D. diss., University of Texas at Austin, 1977.

Examines the writings of both black and white American authors beginning with abolitionist literature through the Harlem Renaissance and ending with the works of James Baldwin. Shows that over time the black female character has become more complex and less type cast.

337. Washington, Mary H. "Teaching Black-Eyed Susans: An Approach to the Study of Black Women Writers." *Black American Literature Forum* 11, no.1 (Spring 1977): 20-24.

Discusses major themes in writings by contemporary black women authors such as black women as suppressed artist. Identifies three cycles in which characters in the literature of

black women can be classified and used for teaching purposes: 1.
the suspended woman (victims of both racial and sexual
oppression). 2. the assimilated woman (assimilated into white
society, but cut-off from their roots). 3. the emergent woman.
The latter refers to the contemporary woman character, a
product of the 1960s.

338. Washington, Mary H., ed. *Black-Eyed Susans: Classic Stories by
      and about Black Women.* New York: Doubleday, 1975.

      A collection of short fiction by black women authors. Each
      selection is introduced with a bio-critical sketch of the author
      outlining major themes in their work. Also includes an
      extensive bibliography.

339. Weems, Renita. "'Artists Without Art Form': A Look at One Black
      Woman's World of Unrevered Black Woman." *Conditions Five* 2,
      no.2 (Autumn 1979): 48-58.

      States that the central theme in Morrison's novels is that
      creative black women are left without outlets for their
      creativity because of the damaging effects of color and gender
      discrimination. Says that men are the cause of tension and
      sorrow in the lives of Morrison's female characters.

340. Wilkerson, Margaret B. "Lorraine Hansberry: The Complete
      Feminist." *Freedomways* 19, no.4 (1979): 235-245.

      Declares that if Hansberry were writing today she would be
      called a feminist because her female characters are central to
      the action of her plays and form the basis for her world-view.

341. Willis, Susan. *Specifying: Black Women Writing the American
      Experience.* Madison, Wisconsin: University of Wisconsin Press,
      1987.

      Includes discussions of the works of Zora Neale Hurston, Paule
      Marshall, Toni Morrison, Alice Walker, and Toni Cade Bambara.
      Willis is interested in the storytelling aspect of the fiction of
      these authors.

342. Wolff, Maria T. "Listening and Living: Reading and Experience in
      *Their Eyes Were Watching God." Black American Literature
      Forum* 16 (Spring 1982): 29-33.

      Asserts that Hurston's novel inspires the reader to interpret the
      text within his or her own experience.

343. Worteck, Susan W. "Forever Free: Art By African-American Women, 1862-1980 An Exhibition." *Feminist Studies* 8 (Spring 1982): 97-108.

    An introduction to and discussion of some of the art works in this exhibition which opened January 30, 1981. Contains eight illustrations from the works in the exhibit.

Social Science

344. Abrahams, Roger D. "Negotiating Respect: Patterns of Presentation Among Black Women." *Journal of American Folklore* 88 (1975): 58-80.

    Studies ways in which black women assert themselves and maintain respect in interpersonal interactions. Uses dialogue from autobiographies and studies by social scientists to gain insight as to how women negotiate respect in the home, among peers, and in male-female interactions.

345. Adams, Kathrynn. "Aspects of Social Context as Determinants of Black Women's Resistance to Challenge." *Journal of Social Issues* 39, no.3 (Fall 1983): 69-78.

    Tested the interaction of race and sex, and how these factors influence resistance to challenges to the opinions of black women. A group of black and white, male and female college students were the subjects of the study. In mixed race, sex pairs they were asked to select the most attractive picture from a group of pictures. Black females were more dominant in defending their opinions with a white partner than white females or black males. This outcome is consistent with the image of the black female as a strong, self-reliant, and independent person.

346. Allen, LaRue, and David W. Britt. "Black Women in American Society: A Resource Development Perspective." *Issues in Mental Health Nursing* 5, no.1-4 (1983): 61-79.

    A review of the social science literature summarizing research studies on black women. Examines the psychological impact of racial, sexual and economic discrimination on black women. Says that despite triple discrimination, black women survive because they are able to marshal economic, personal and social resources to combat stress. Family relationships and friendships with other women help them cope with stress.

347. Ball, Richard E. "Expressive Functioning and the Black Family: Life and Domain Satisfaction of Black Women." Ph.D. diss., The University of Florida, 1980.

Assesses the impact of marital status on overall life satisfaction and satisfaction with family life and children of 373 black women. Concludes that satisfaction levels were as high for the widowed and the divorced as for the married. However, single and separated had lower life satisfaction levels.

348.   Ball, Richard E. "Friendship Networks: More Supportive of Low-Income Black Women?" *Ethnicity* 7, no.1 (March 1980): 70-77.

Examined the significance of friendship support networks in the lives of low-income black females as compared to low-income white females. No statistically significant difference was found between the two groups of women with regard to number of friends, contact with them, or perceived potential helpfulness. However, results of the study showed that blacks made fewer requests for aid than did the white females. The contention that black women have more highly developed friendship networks was not supported by the data.

349.   Benjamin, Lois. "Black Women Achievers: An Isolated Elite." *Sociological Inquiry* 52, no.2 (Spring 1982): 141-151.

A study of black career women and their views of mate selection and marriage. The author interviewed fifty-four female subjects and classified them into two types according to their attitudes towards marriage. Type A women were interested in the traditional goals of marriage and motherhood while type B women had less dependency on men for identity and were more career committed than type A women.

350.   Binton, Victoria J. "An Analysis of Factors Influencing the Development of Sex Role Identity and Sex Role Attitudes of Contemporary Black Women." Ph.D. diss., University of Michigan, 1981.

Found that black women tend to be more androgynous than white women, and androgynous black women had more self-esteem and lower levels of anxiety and depression.

351.   Brown, Anita et al. "A Review of Psychology of Women Textbooks: Focus on the Afro-American Woman." *Psychology of Women Quarterly* 9 (March 1985): 29-38.

Reviewed twenty-eight books, of which eighteen offered token or no references to Afro-American women. Authors conclude that race and class bias are responsible for this exclusion and Euro-American middle-class women's experiences are regarded as representing the experiences of all American women.

352. Brown, Delindus R. "Survey of the Black Woman and the Persuasion Process." *Journal of Black Studies* 9, no.2 (December 1978): 233-248.

    Identifies two strategies of communication (identification and resistance) which combine to form a unique technique of persuasion. Uses this theory to analyze some of the actions of black women throughout American history and in the contemporary black women's movement.

353. Brown, Shirley V. "Early Childbearing and Poverty: Implications for Social Services." *Adolescence* 17, no.66 (Summer 1982): 397-408.

    Asserts that public social services are not providing black and Hispanic teenage parents with services such as homemaking and child care skills, contraceptive services, education and employment skills that would help them avoid poverty.

354. Bryant, Barbara H. "The Postdivorce Adjustment of Middle Class Black Women." D.S.W. diss., University of California, Los Angeles, 1982.

    This is a study of divorce rates among a non-probability sampling of sixty black women between the ages of twenty-one to sixty-seven years of age.

355. Coe, Sherri N. "A Study of Identity Patterns Among Three Generations of Black Women." Ph.D. diss., Northwestern University, 1982.

    A study of the psychological development, values, and self-views of three generations of black women. For the oldest generation, survival was the basic life principle. Upward mobility was the most important life principle for the second generation, and personal mobility was the governing life factor for the youngest generation.

356. Coleman, Gardner, and Jacquelyn Lea. "A Comparative Study of the Assertiveness of Black and White Women at the University Level." Ph.D. diss., Southern Illinois University at Carbondale, 1977.

    The goal of this study was to ascertain if there is a correlation between attractiveness and level of assertiveness for black and white college women. No empirical evidence was uncovered to support the hypothesis that there is a difference in assertiveness between black and white women.

357. Dougherty, Molly C. *Becoming a Woman in Rural Black Culture.* New York: Holt, Rinehart and Winston, 1978.

An anthropological case study of a rural southern black
community which focuses on life cycle passages of women. Says
motherhood is an important event which provides women with
elevated status in this community.

358. Fleming, Jacqueline. "Fear of Success in Black Male and Female
      Graduate Students: A Pilot Study." *Psychology of Women
      Quarterly* 6, no.3 (Spring 1982): 327-341.

      A preliminary study of the motive to avoid success in black men
      and women. Fourteen female and twenty-one male graduate
      students at Harvard University were tested. Evidence of
      success avoidance was not shown in either sex.

359. Franklin, Clyde W. "Black Male-Black Female Conflict: Individually
      Caused and Culturally Nurtured." *Journal of Black Studies* 15,
      no.2 (December 1984): 139-154.

      Examines role conflict between contemporary black males and
      females. States that most authors believe this conflict to be
      destructive and potentially explosive. Identifies two sources of
      the problem: 1. Sex roles internalized as children by black males
      and females are noncomplemetary. 2. Structural barriers such as
      higher unemployment, high incidence of drug addiction and
      incarceration result in a scarcity of socially functional black
      men.

360. Gary, Robenia B. "Black Women and Their Utilization Experiences
      with Public Agencies." D.S.W. diss., University of Pennsylvania,
      1983.

      An investigation of how demographic and socio-cultural factors
      affect use of public welfare agencies and satisfaction with these
      services among black women in the United States. Findings
      indicated that the more contact a woman had with a public
      agency the less she was satisfied with the services provided.

361. Gaston, John C. "The Acculturation of the First-Generation Black
      Professional Woman: A Denver, Colorado Area Study." *Western
      Journal of Black Studies* 4, no.4 (Winter 1980): 256-260.

      Looks at the expectations for male-female relationships of first
      generation black professional women in the Denver area. A
      majority of the participants had a positive image of the black
      male, but some of their comments indicate a feeling of
      ambivalence towards the black male.

362. Gatz, Margaret et al. "Psychosocial Competence Characteristics of
      Black and White Women: The Constraining Effects of 'Triple
      Jeopardy.'" *The Black Scholar* 13 (January-February 1982): 5-12.

Compared a sample of black and white older women with a
similar sample of black and white adolescent females to test
their ability to cope with discrimination based on race, sex, and
age. Older women of color scored especially high on the ability
to cope with the adverse effects of discrimination.

363. Griffin, Jean T. "Black Women's Experience as Authority Figures in
Groups." *Women's Studies Quarterly* 14, no.1 and 2
(Spring/Summer 1986): 7-12.

Used black women as leaders of employee training groups to
observe the reactions of white males to black women in roles of
authority. Over half of the initial reactions were negative and
included behaviors such as challenging the expertise of the black
female trainers or denying her presence. However, as a result
of the training experience, the trainers felt that participants
became more positive about the credibility of black women in
leadership positions.

364. Gump, Janice P. "Comparative Analysis of Black Women's and
White Women's Sex Role Attitudes." *Journal of Consulting and
Clinical Psychology* 43, no.6 (1975): 858-863.

An empirical study which assessed the sex role attitudes of
seventy-seven black college women and forty white college
women. In comparison to white women, black women were
found to be more submissive and to define their identity in the
roles of wife and mother. Gump surmises that this may be a
reaction to the popular image of black women as matriarchs.
White women, on the other hand, expressed more interest in
fulfilling nontraditional roles such a attending graduate schools.
The author says that over time white women have become more
achievement oriented.

365. Howell, C. Diane. "Black Concepts of the Ideal Black Woman."
Ph.D. diss., University of California, Berkeley, 1978.

Researched qualities of the ideal black woman as perceived by
black men and women, and found that both sexes agree on these
qualities.

366. Jackson, Agnes D. "Militancy and Black Women's Competitive
Behavior in Competitive Versus Noncompetitive Conditions."
Psychology of Women Quarterly 6, no.3 (Spring 1982): 342-353.

In this study a militancy scale was used to measure the degree
of concern with the struggle for black liberation of one hundred
single black female undergraduates. Subjects were given anagram tests to work under both competitive and noncompetitive
conditions. The outcome indicated that the highly militant

students working in competitive conditions worked for longer
periods of time, produced more words from the anagram, and
felt more self-confident.

367. Jackson, Jacqueline J. "The Plight of the Older Black Woman in
      the United States." *The Black Scholar* 7 (April 1976): 47-54.

      Uses census data to assess the situation of aging black women.
      Specifically addresses the topics of economics, loneliness,
      mortality, and isolation. The author found that in general the
      conditions under which Afro-American women live merely become
      more exacerbated in old age.

368. Jewell, Karen. "An Analysis of the Visual Development of a
      Stereotype: The Media's Portrayal of 'Mammy' and 'Aunt Jemima'
      as Symbols of Black Womanhood." Ph.D. diss., Ohio State
      University, 1976.

      Explores the development of the above stereotypes in the mass
      media from an historical perspective. Looks at the sociological
      implications of these images on the treatment of American black
      women, and concludes that they have been generalized to all
      black women.

369. Lewis, Shelby. "The Meaning and Effect of the UN Decade for
      Women on Black Women in America." *Women's Studies
      International Forum* 8, no.2 (1985): 117-120.

      This study is based on interviews with thirty black women
      activists from different educational and occupational backgrounds
      and various regions of the United States. Says that the masses
      of black women are inadequately informed about the UN Decade
      and thus, are excluded from participation in it.

370. Lykes, M. Brinton. "Discrimination and Coping in the Lives of
      Black Women." *Journal of Social Issues* 39, no.3 (1983): 79-100.

      Examines the individual and combined effects of racist and
      sexist oppression on the lives of black women and the coping
      strategies they used to confront these situations. Findings
      suggest that directly challenging discrimination may be less
      effective than less direct, more creative coping strategies.

371. Murray, Saundra R., and Martha T.S. Mednick. "Black Women's
      Achievement Orientation: Motivational and Cognitive Factors."
      Psychology of Women Quarterly 1, no.3 (Spring 1977): 247-259.

      A review of the literature concerning achievement motivation
      and fear of success in black women. Notes inconclusiveness of

research findings, and provides suggestions for possible future
research directions.

372.   Myers, Lena W. "Black Women and Self-Esteem." in *Another Voice:
       Feminist Perspectives on Social Life and Social Science.* Edited
       by Marcia Millman and Rosabeth M. Kanter. New York:
       Doubleday, 1975, pp. 240-250.

       An investigation of the level of self-esteem of black women in
       matriarchally structured families. Concludes that families headed
       by women do not contribute to lowering the self-esteem of
       women of color, and proposes that the white, middle-class model
       of family life should not be the standard by which black women
       are evaluated.

373.   Myers, Lena W. *Black Women, Do They Cope Better?* Englewood
       Cliffs, New Jersey: Prentice-Hall, 1980.

       A comparative study of the coping mechanisms of black women
       Compared Afro-American women who were single heads of
       families with black women who had mates. The sample consisted
       of two hundred women from Grand Rapids, Michigan and two
       hundred from Jackson, Mississippi. Myers found that single
       black women who are heads of households coped as well as
       married black women.

374.   Pugh, Clementine A. "Psychological Dimensions of Masculinity and
       Femininity and Attitudes Toward Women Among Black, Hispanic,
       and White Female College Students." Ed.D. diss., University of
       Massachusetts, 1982.

       Sampled 139 black, 145 Hispanic, and 123 white female college
       students to compare self-reports of masculinity and femininity.
       Also studied perceptions of the "ideal" man and woman of their
       own racial/ethnic group. All three groups of women responded
       differently on all the measures which was attributed to
       racial/ethnic differences.

375.   Rosen, Raye H. "Sex Role Attitudes of Black And White Women."
       International Journal of Women's Studies 1 (November-December
       1978): 544-554.

       Reports the results of a study which compared and contrasted
       the attitudes of black and white women to the female role. In
       addition, the author was interested in determining the extent of
       traditionality or nontraditionality in areas such as work roles,
       family roles, and sex roles. The population studied were from
       the working class and were employed in low-level occupations.
       Results showed that black women were more traditional than or

did not differ from white women with regard to women's friendship, work roles, and sexual roles.

376. Smith, Althea. "Nonverbal Communication Among Black Female Dyads: An Assessment of Intimacy, Gender and Race." *Journal of Social Issues* 39, no.3 (1983): 55-67.

Analyzed the frequency of three nonverbal cues (smiling, looking, and leaning) obtained from observation of randomly selected same sex couples in a fast food eating establishment. The behavior of black women was compared to white women and black men. Concludes that black women should not be lumped together with all women or all blacks since their nonverbal behavior may be different than any other group.

377. Watts Jones, Danielle L. "The Quality of Social Support Among African-American Women and its Effect as a Mediator of the Relationship Between Stress and Depression." Ph.D. diss., Duke University, 1984.

Watts interviewed black women to determine events in their lives which caused stress. The Black Woman's Stressor List was compiled from these interviews. Phase II of the study was concerned with evaluating if social support among African-American women served as a buffer between stress and the outcome of depression. The results were negative.

CHAPTER 2

ASIAN AMERICAN WOMEN

This chapter includes materials about Chinese, Japanese, Korean, and Filipino American women. Although, the literature on Asian American women is less extensive than that of black women it has been growing in the last few years. This is an area in which more scholarship is needed.

Chinese and Japanese women were first brought to the United States to work as prostitutes in the nineteenth century. They were radically outnumbered by their male counterparts who had journeyed to America to earn money and return home to China or Japan. There are a number of research articles describing the situation of these women.

After 1900 and until the early 1920s Japanese and Korean women traveled to Hawaii and the continental United States to marry men from their own countries who were working in the United States. These women are referred to as picture brides because they had not met their husbands before the trip to America. Their marriages were arranged in Japan or Korea and they had only seen their prospective spouse in a photograph. There are some excellent life histories of these women.

After World War II immigration laws were liberalized and greater numbers of Asian women traveled to the United States. Some of these women came into the country as the wives of servicemen. There are a few studies on the problems of adjustment encountered by Asian war brides.

Scholarly studies discussing employment and economic issues comprise a large portion of the literature of Asian American women. Most notable of these is the work of Evelyn Nakano Glenn who has studied employment patterns of three generations of Japanese women in the United States.

Several works focus on the problems of acculturation into American society of second and third-generation Asian American women. Autobiographical works such as Maxine Hong Kingston's *The Woman Warrior* and Jeanne Wakatsuki Houston's *Farewell to Manzanar* reflect the conflicts of growing up as an Asian female in a white, male world. Also, there are a number of psychological and sociological studies dealing with the development of self-concept in second and third generation Asian American women.

General Works

378.   Kumagai, Gloria L. "The Asian Woman in America." *Explorations in Ethnic Studies* 1 (July 1978): 27-39.

Presents an overview of the history and present status of Asian American women in the United States. Says there is a need for information on Asian American women to be made available in educational institutions.

*   See also item 305.

379.   Tsuchida, Nobuya, ed. *Asian and Pacific American Experiences: Women's Perspectives*. Minneapolis, Minn.: Asian/Pacific American Learning Resource Center, University of Minnesota, 1982.

Contains a diverse collection of essays, conference papers, interviews, and testimonies by and/or about Japanese American, Filipino American, and Indochinese American women. Contains items 399, 416 and 417.

380.   Young, Judy et al. "Asian-American Women: A Bibliography." *Bridge: An Asian American Perspective* 6, no.4 (Winter 1978): 49-53.

Lists periodicals, books, anthologies, and articles which are readily available at the Asian Community Library (Oakland Public Library) and the Asian American Studies Library (University of California, Berkeley) on the subject.

Autobiography, Biography, Life Histories

381.   Chai, Alice Y. "A Picture Bride from Korea: The Life History of a Korean American Woman in Hawaii." *Bridge: An Asian American Perspective* 6 (Winter 1978): 37-42.

This is the life story of a Korean picture bride who came to Hawaii to marry a man she had never met. Her husband was a laborer and she had to do ironing to supplement the family income. Eventually she was able to start her own business as the proprietor of a boardinghouse.

382.   Choy, Bong Y. *Koreans in America*. Chicago, Illinois: Nelson-Hall, 1979.

This collection of oral histories of elderly Koreans in the United States contains several biographies of women including the memoirs of picture brides and a woman who was a social worker in San Francisco's Chinatown.

383. Chua, Cheng L. "Golden Mountain: Chinese Versions of the American Dream in Lin Yutang, Louis Chu, and Maxine Hong Kingston." *Ethnic Groups* 4, no.1-2 (1982): 33-59.

    Discusses the opposite images of womanhood presented in *The Woman Warrior* through which Kingston searches for her own identity. Says that it represents Kingston's attempt to center herself as a Chinese American, a woman, and a writer.

384. Houston, Jeanne W. *Farewell to Manzanar: A True Story of Japanese American Experience During and After the World War II Internment.* Boston: Houghton Mifflin, 1973.

    A biographical novel based on the experiences of the author and her family in the internment camp of Manzanar, California.

385. Hsu, Vivian. "Maxine Hong Kingston as Psycho-Autobiographer and Ethnographer." *International Journal of Women's Studies* 6, no.5 (November-December 1983): 429-442.

    Hsu believes that *The Woman Warrior* was written as an act of self-realization, and she says that because it deals with the author's own psychic experiences, it can be considered a psycho-autobiography. She also sees it as reflective of the experiences common to all Chinese Americans and, thus, she characterizes it as an ethnography. A valuable aid in interpreting a very complex work. Should be read in conjunction with *The Woman Warrior.*

386. Kim, Elaine. "Visions and Fierce Dreams: A Commentary on the Works of Maxine Hong Kingston." *Amerasia* 8, no.2 (1981): 145-161.

    Offers an in-depth explication of *The Woman Warrior.* Sees the book as an attempt by the author to sort fantasy from reality in her childhood experiences in order to come to terms with the contradictions that shaped her life as a member of a minority group and a female in America. An excellent companion piece to Kingston's work.

387. Kim, Elaine. *With Silk Wings: Asian American Women at Work.* San Francisco, Calif.: Asian American Women United of California, 1983.

    Part I contains brief life stories of twelve Asian American women who have achieved successful careers. Part II profiles forty women working in a wide range of occupations, and Part III is a brief history of Chinese, Japanese, Korean, and Filipino women in the United States.

388. Kingston, Maxine H. *The Woman Warrior: Memoirs of a Girlhood Among Ghosts.* New York: Knopf, dist. by Random House, 1976.

An autobiographical work in which Kingston reflects on her experiences growing up in the United States as the eldest daughter of Chinese immigrants. This is a highly acclaimed, but complex book which blends elements of myth, fantasy, and autobiography. In it, Kingston attempts to come to grips with the contradictions of her childhood such as the fact that her mother is a strong independent woman, but, at the same time, Maxine is reminded by here mother that girls are useless.

389. Koga, Claire. "Issei Woman: An Oral History." *Asian American Women* 1 (May 1976): 17-17.

Tells the story of Mrs. Imakire who came with her husband to the United States in 1919. Relates her difficulty with learning English and the long hours she worked operating a boarding-house in Palo Alto, California in the early years of her marriage.

390. McCunn, Ruthanne L. *Thousand Pieces of Gold: A Biographical Novel.* San Francisco, California: Design Enterprises of San Francisco, 1981.

An historical novel based on the life of Lalu Nathoy, later known as Polly Bemis. The author conducted extensive research using private papers, newspapers, journals and oral histories on which this account is based. In China Lalu was sold by her father to a bandit for two bags of seed. Then, she was shipped to America and sold as a slave girl to a wealthy Chinese saloon keeper in the mining camp of Warrens, Idaho. With the help of Charlie Bemis, whom she later married, she was able to obtain her freedom and start her own business. Throughout her long life she was highly respected by her neighbors for her medical skills.

391. "Mary Tsukamota." in *Dignity: Lower Income Women Tell of Their Lives and Struggles.* Edited by Fran Leeper Buss. Ann Arbor, Michigan: University of Michigan Press, 1985, pp. 85-109.

This is the life story of the daughter of Japanese immigrants. She discusses her mother's experience as a young bride who traveled from Japan to California in 1910 and her family's struggle to earn a living in the United States. She relates her encounters with prejudice and the chaos created in the Japanese community by the evacuation order during World War II.

392. "Maxine Hong Kingston." in *Women Writers of the West Coast*. Edited by Arturo Islas and Marilyn Yalon. Santa Barbara, Calif.: Capra Press, 1983, pp. 11-19.

   A brief interview in which Kingston discusses how her background affects her writings.

393. Shimada, Charlene. "America Must Be Like Heaven." *Asian American Women* 1 (May 1976): 8-12.

   An oral history of Eufemia Genetiano who came to the United States from the Philippines as a war bride after World War II. She tells of her expectations for life in America and relates the realities of her life which consisted of hard work as a maid and raising a large family.

394. Sunoo, Sonia S. "Korean Women Pioneers of the Pacific Northwest." *Oregon Historical Quarterly* 79 (Spring 1978): 51-63.

   Presents the stories of six Korean American women who emigrated to Oregon and Montana between 1910 and 1924 under the picture bride system in which they married men they had seen only through a photograph. A common element in all of their lives was hard work, suffering, and disappointment--not at all what they had expected.

395. Tanaka, Michiko. *Through Harsh Winters: The Life of a Japanese Immigrant Woman*. Novato, California: Chandler and Sharp, 1981.

   This is the life story of an *issei* woman which has been translated from Japanese by her daughter, Akemi Kikumura. Michiko Tanaka came with her husband to Liberty in Northern California as a bride in 1923. Born into a wealthy family in Japan, her living conditions worsened in America. She was required to cook for the men in the labor camp where her husband was employed. She worked in the fields with her husband moving from camp to camp. She says that work outside the home allowed her a sense of equality with her husband.

396. Wong, Jade S. *No Chinese Stranger*. New York: Harper and Row, 1975.

   The continuation of Wong's autobiography begun twenty-five years earlier with *Fifth Chinese Daughter*. This volume describes the author's adult years in which she marries, has children, and establishes her career as a designer of pottery and ceramics.

397. Wunsch, Marie A. "Walls of Jade: Images of Men, Women and
      Family in Second Generation Asian-American Fiction and
      Autobiography." Ph.D. diss., University of Hawaii, 1977.

      Analyzes autobiographical writings by second-generation Chinese,
      Japanese, and Korean American writers including works by
      Maxine Hong Kingston and Jeanne Wakatsuki Houston. Sees
      these works as illustrative of the transition between the
      immigrant generation and the acculturation of the second
      generation. Says that of all the authors analyzed here, only
      Kingston makes an attempt to portray a female character who
      shows a deeper understanding of the limited roles assigned
      women in both Chinese and American cultures.

Education and Employment

398. Aquino, Belinda. "The History of Filipino Women in Hawaii."
      Bridge: An Asian American Perspective 7 (Spring 1979): 17-21.

      Traces employment patterns of Filipino women in Hawaii from
      the early twentieth century until the present time. Says that
      the main problem facing recent immigrants is the need to
      retrain in order to qualify for professional licenses.

399. Aquino, Belinda. "Occupational Mobility of Filipino Women Workers
      in Hawaii." in *Asian and Pacific American Experiences: Women's
      Perspectives*. Edited by Nobudja Tsuchida. Minneapolis, Minn.:
      Asian/Pacific American Learning Resource Center, University of
      Minnesota, 1982, pp. 127-137.

      A study based on census data and oral interviews of the
      employment patterns of Filipino women in Hawaii. It is
      primarily concerned with the period after 1950 when increasing
      numbers of Filipinos entered the labor force. Concludes that
      most women in the study are confined to the blue collar/service
      occupations, and upward mobility is limited due to limited
      political influence and racial discrimination.

400. Chu, Lily. "Asian-American Women in Educational Research."
      Integrated Education 18, no.5-6 (Sept.-Dec. 1980): 55-60.

      Asserts that Asian American women are underrepresented in the
      field of educational research, and that this is due largely to
      language and cultural barriers. Recommends the need for special
      training in assertiveness and public speaking skills, social skills,
      job acquisition skills, and career awareness skills for young
      Asian American women.

401. Cordova, Dorothy L. "Educational Alternatives for Asian/Pacific Women." in *Conference on the Educational and Occupational Needs of Asian-Pacific American Women*. Washington D.C.: The National Institute of Education, 1980, pp. 135-156.

Identifies lack of English proficiency as one of the main obstacles to career advancement of Asian American women which prevents them from translating their professional skills into equivalent professional jobs in the United States. Consequently, they are forced to take lower paying jobs.

402. Fong, Eva C. "Barriers to Educational Leadership Aspirations as Perceived by California Asian American Women Administrators." Ed.D. diss., University of the Pacific, 1984.

Examines barriers to career advancement of Asian American women in educational administration. One hundred and thirty-one women of Japanese and Chinese ancestry were surveyed. Their heritage as Asian Americans was not considered to be a barrier to career advancement by the participants of this study.

403. Fong, Pauline, and Amado Y. Cabezas. "Economic and Employment Status of Asian-Pacific Women." in *Conference on the Educational and Occupational Needs of Asian-Pacific American Women*. Washington D.C.: The National Institute of Education, 1980, pp. 255-321.

The authors of this study conclude that although more Asian American women work than white women, their earning power is low relative to their educational and occupational levels. States that Asian-heritage women tend to concentrate in traditional female occupations and avoid jobs requiring public contact or high language facility. Suggests that ways to broaden career choices should be investigated.

404. Fong, Pauline, and Amado Cabezas. "Selected Statistics on the Status of Asian-American Women." *Amerasia Journal* 4, no.1 (1977): 133-142.

Presents some preliminary data taken from the 1970 census on labor force participation, earnings, occupational distribution, and educational levels for Chinese, Japanese and Filipino women living in the San Francisco Bay Area.

405. Fukuda, Kimiko A. "Chinese American and Japanese American
      Women in California Public School Administration." Ed.D. diss.,
      University of Southern California, 1984.

      Structured interviews with forty-seven Asian American women
      administrators were used to collect data for this study. The
      participants indicated that stereotypes of Asian American women
      as quiet and submissive make it difficult for them to become
      leaders and administrators.

406. Glenn, Evelyn N. "The Dialectics of Wage Work: Japanese-American
      Women and Domestic Service, 1905-1940." *Feminist Studies* 6,
      no.3 (Fall 1980): 432-471.

      See item 407.

407. Glenn, Evelyn N. *Issei, Nisei, War Bride: Three Generations of
      Japanese American Women in Domestic Service.* Philadelphia,
      Pa.: Temple University Press, 1986.

      A study based on oral interviews of Japanese American women
      employed as domestics in the San Francisco Bay Area during the
      first seventy years of the twentieth century. Glenn focuses on
      labor market segmentation by race, gender, and migrant status,
      and she compares the struggles of these women in the work
      place with their situation in the home. She says Japanese
      American women were forced into a narrow segment of the
      labor market (domestic service) because of their race, gender,
      and immigrant status.

408. Glenn, Evelyn N. "Occupational Ghettoization: Japanese American
      Women and Domestic Service, 1905-1970." *Ethnicity* 8, no.4
      (1981): 352-386.

      See item 407.

409. Leonetti, Donna L., and Laura Newell-Morris. "Lifetime Patterns of
      Childbearing and Employment: A Study of Second-Generation
      Japanese American Women." *Journal of Bio-Social Science* 14,
      no.1 (January 1982): 81-98.

      Investigated lifetime patterns of fertility in relationship to
      outside employment in second-generation Japanese American
      women. Retrospective longitudinal data over a period of
      approximately sixty years was examined. The patterns
      documented in this study reflect a lifetime process of
      integration of childbearing and child rearing with employment.
      The authors suggest this is a result of post-World War II
      unemployment and underemployment of Japanese American men.

410. Navarro, Jovina. "Immigration of Filipino Women to America." *Asian American Women* 1 (May 1976): 18-22.

This article looks at the shortage of females to males among Filipino farm workers in the United States during the period before the Second World War. Says that during the 1970s Filipino women entered the United States labor force largely through economic necessity.

411. Wong, Morrison G., and Charles Hirschman. "Labor Force Participation and Socioeconomic Attainment of Asian American Women." *Sociological Perspectives* 26, no.4 (October 1983): 423-446.

Using data from the 1970 census, compares the socioeconomic roles and labor force participation of Asian American women to Anglo women. Differentiates between native-born and foreign-born women. Asserts that Asian American women earn more than Anglo women due to superior educational qualifications, greater levels of full-time work, and geographical location in metropolitan areas which are conducive to labor market participation.

412. Woo, Deborah. "The Socioeconomic Status of Asian American Women in the Labor Force: An Alternative View." *Sociological Perspectives* 28, no.3 (July 1985): 307-338.

A rejoinder to the 1983 article by Wong and Hirschman (see item 411). Argues that Asian American women do not earn higher incomes than Anglo women. Says that Asian American women gain less from their educational efforts than do white women or men. States that more Asian women than white women are employed due to economic necessity (i.e. to supplement the income of their husbands which is lower relative to the income of white males).

Feminism and Women's Studies

413. Chai, Alice Y. "Toward a Holistic Paradigm for Asian American Women's Studies: A Synthesis of Feminist Scholarship and Women of Color's Feminist Politics." *Women's Studies International Forum* 8, no.1 (1985): 59-66.

Advocates a holistic paradigm to women's studies curriculum on Third World women, using the example of Asian American women, to emphasize the inter-connectedness of sexism, racism, classism, ageism, disableism, and homophobia in the American social system. Says that women of color and white feminists should work together in each other's organizations to build a larger community of sisterhood.

414. Loo, Chalsa, and Ong, Paul. "Slaying Demons with a Sewing
      Needle: Feminist Issues for Chinatown's Women." *Berkeley
      Journal of Sociology* 27 (1982): 77-88.

      This study based on face-to-face interviews with 108 female
      residents in San Francisco's Chinatown outlines some of the
      major problems facing these women such as low self-esteem,
      lack of educational and occupational mobility, and lack of
      assertiveness and a sense of control over the outcomes in their
      lives. Says that although the women of Chinatown could benefit
      from the women's movement there are too many barriers of
      race, culture, and class which prevent their integration into the
      movement.

  *   See also item 175.

415. Wong, Germain Q. "Impediments to Asian-Pacific-American Women
      Organizing." in *Conference on the Educational and Occupational
      Needs of Asian-Pacific American Women*. Washington D.C.: The
      National Institute of Education, 1980, pp. 89-103.

      Discusses some of the barriers which have prevented Asian/
      Pacific American women from participating more actively in the
      women's movement. Says that the primary obstacle is the
      centuries of cultural conditioning which relegates women from
      Asian countries to an inferior status. States that Asian
      American women are more likely to join organizations concerned
      with liberating their own ethnic groups rather than white
      feminist organizations and if they do join feminist causes, it is
      within their own ethnic group.

History

416. Chai, Alice Y. "Korean Women in Hawaii, 1903-1945." in *Asian and
      Pacific American Experiences: Women's Perspectives*. Edited by
      Nobuya Tsuchida. Minneapolis, Minn.: Asian/Pacific American
      Learning Resource Center, University of Minnesota, 1982, pp.
      75-87.

      Traces the history of Korean immigrant women in Hawaii with
      special attention to their participation in the Korean
      independence movement.

417. Hirata, Lucie. "Chinese Immigrant Women in Nineteenth-Century
      California." in *Asian and Pacific American Experiences: Women's
      Perspectives*. Edited by Nobuya Tsuchida. Minneapolis, Minn.:
      Asian/Pacific American Learning Resource Center, University of
      Minnesota, 1982, pp. 38-55.

Uses census data to describe the occupations of immigrant women in nineteenth-century California.

418. Hirata, Lucie. "Free, Indentured, Enslaved: Chinese Prostitutes in Nineteenth-Century America." *Signs: Journal of Women in Culture and Society* 5, no.1 (Autumn 1979): 3-29.

This is a social history of Chinese prostitution in nineteenth-century California. Says prostitution was a form of labor which grew out of the distressed conditions in China and served the largely male population of Chinese laborers. States that prostitutes were ruthlessly exploited and were victims of white racism and Chinese patriarchy. One of the most in-depth accounts of the subject.

419. Ichioka, Yuji. "*Amerika Nadeshiko*: Japanese Immigrant Women in the United States, 1900-1924." *Pacific Historical Review* 49, no.2 (May 1980): 339-357.

Based on group discussions with retired first-generation Japanese American women and immigrant press accounts, this article examines the picture bride system and its effect on immigrant society. It portrays a realistic account of the hardships and disillusionment encountered by Japanese immigrant women.

420. Ichioka, Yuji. "Ameyuki-san: Japanese Prostitutes in Nineteenth-Century America." *Amerasia Journal* 4, no.1 (1977): 1-21.

A study of the first female immigrants to come to America from Japan. Says that though they were fewer in number than their Chinese Counterparts, they were as equally downtrodden.

421. Kataoka, Susan M. "Issei Women: A Study in Subordinate Status." Ph.D. diss., University of California, Los Angeles, 1977.

A study of first generation Japanese American immigrant women. Examines such topics as reasons for emigrating and the subordinate status of these women based on race and sex discrimination.

422. Matsumoto, Valerie. "Japanese American Women During World War II." *Frontiers* 8, no.1 (1984): 6-14.

Focuses on the experiences of second-generation Japanese American women during the years of the Second World War. It is based on oral interviews, letters of internees, census records, and relocation camp newspapers. Says that the relocation camp experience brought about disintegration of traditional arranged marriages, equal pay with men for working women, and new

opportunities for travel, work, and education for the younger
women internees.

423. Wong, Joyce M. "Prostitution: San Francisco Chinatown, Mid-and
      Late-Nineteenth Century." *Bridge: An Asian American Perspective*
      6 (Winter 1978): 23-28.

      Lays the blame for prostitution in Chinatown on the poor
      economic conditions in nineteenth-century China and the low
      position of women in Chinese society. Asserts that Chinese
      prostitutes were harassed more often than white prostitutes.

424. Young, Judy. "'A Bowlful of Tears:' Chinese American Women
      Immigrants on Angel Island." *Frontiers* 2, no.2 (Summer 1977):
      52-55.

      This is an account of the hardships faced by Chinese immigrant
      women who were detained on Angel Island. It is based on
      interviews with the women involved and some of the immigration
      officials who worked on the island during the 1920s.

425. Young, Judy. *Chinese Women of America: A Pictorial History*.
      Seattle, Washington: University of Washington Press (for the
      Chinese Cultural Foundation of San Francisco), 1986.

      This book is based on a traveling exhibit of photographs,
      "Chinese Women of America, 1834-1982." One hundred and
      thirty-five photos from the exhibit were selected for inclusion
      in this work. Together, the text and the pictures provide an
      interesting account of the role and accomplishments of Chinese
      American women in the United States.

Social Science

426. Abramson, Paul R., and John Imai-Marquez. "The Japanese-
      American: A Cross-Cultural Study of Sex Guilt." *Journal of
      Research in Personality* 16, no.2 (June 1982): 227-237.

      An examination of three generations of Japanese Americans and
      matched Caucasian American controls. Results of the study
      confirm the hypothesis that women of the first generation of
      Japanese Americans display more sex guilt than any of the other
      groups, but says attitudes about human sexuality have liberalized
      across the three generations. However, Japanese American
      women still express the highest levels of sex guilt of the
      samples assessed.

427. Armstrong, M. Jocelyn. "Ethnicity and Sex-Role Socialization: A
      Comparative Example Using Life History Data from Hawaii." *Sex
      Roles* 10, no.3/4 (1984): 157-181.

Life history data collected from two Hawaiian women, one from the Chinese community and the other from the Portuguese community, are compared in order to research the impact of ethnicity on the learning of female sex roles.

428. Braun, Jean S., and Hilda A. Chao. "Attitudes Toward Women: A Comparison of Asian-Born Chinese and American Caucasians." *Psychology of Women Quarterly* 2, no.3 (Spring 1978): 195-201.

This study compares the attitude towards women of Asian-born Chinese Americans and Caucasian Americans. The Spence-Helmrich Attitudes Toward Women Scale was used to test both males and females. The authors hypothesized that the Chinese Americans would be more liberal in their views of women's roles. However, this was not confirmed by the results of the study. The outcome of the research indicated that Chinese-born women were more conservative than Caucasian females or Chinese-born males.

429. Chow, Esther N.L. "The Acculturation Experience of Asian American Women." in *Beyond Sex Roles*. 2nd ed. Edited by Alice G. Sargent. San Francisco, Calif.: West Publishing Co., 1985, pp. 238-251.

Examines the triple bind of race, sex, and class status imposed on Asian American women and its effect on the development of self-concept. Says Asian culture tends to reinforce traditional feminine traits such as submissiveness, passivity, altruism and timidness. Asserts that Asian families discourage females from forming high self-esteem or individuality.

430. Connor, John W. *A Study of the Marital Stability of Japanese War Brides*. San Francisco, Calif.: R and E Research Associates, 1976.

A scholarly study of the marital adjustment of twenty racially mixed couples living in the Sacramento area. Results of the study indicated that the couples were relatively well-adjusted.

431. Filmore, Lily W., and Jacqueline L. Cheong. "The Early Socialization of Asian-American Female Children." in *Conference on the Educational and Occupational Needs of Asian-Pacific American Women*. Washington, D.C.: National Institute of Education, 1980, pp. 237-253.

This study is based on interviews with several first and second-generation Chinese American women. The discussions revealed that all the informants experienced conflicts between the secondary female role for which they were socialized and their aspirations for independent careers. Concludes that Asian

American women are raised with a built-in success inhibitor which acts as a barrier to independent achievement.

432. Iu, Carol R. "Ethnic and Economic correlates of Marital Satisfaction and Attitude Towards Divorce of Chinese American Women." D.S.W. diss., University of California, Los Angeles, 1982.

Eighty-two American-born Chinese women living in the Los Angeles area were interviewed for this study. The subjects were all married to Chinese American men. The independent variables were the subjects' level of ethnic identity and economic independence. Results indicated that those women who had a strong ethnic identity had a more conservative opinion about divorce and were more likely not to choose divorce as a solution to marital conflict. On the other hand, those women who were more economically independent were more likely to consider divorce as an alternative.

433. Kim, Bok-Lim C. "Asian Wives of U.S. Servicemen: Women in Shadows." *Amerasia Journal* 4, no.1 (1977): 91-115.

A study of the problems of acculturation of the Korean and Japanese wives of U.S. serviceman. Kim asserts that very few social services exist to provide help for these women, and she recommends that bilingual/bicultural training and orientation classes should be mandatory before and after arrival of the women in the United States.

434. Kim, Jean. "Processes of Asian American Identity Development: A Study of Japanese American Women's Perceptions of Their Struggle to Achieve Positive Identities as Americans of Asian Ancestry." Ed.D. diss., University of Massachusetts, 1981.

In this study ten third-generation Japanese American women were interviewed in order to determine the process of identity formation in Asian American women and how they resolved conflicts between their racial heritage and the dominant white society. The outcome of the research suggested that individuals progress through five stages of development until the conflict is resolved and a positive racial identity as Asian Americans is achieved.

435. Louie, Belser. "Characteristics of Asian American Student/Clients." Ph.D. diss., The Wright Institute, 1979.

The counseling needs of male and female Chinese American and Japanese American students were examined in this study. Data was used from the counseling center of the University of California at Berkeley. Significant differences between the two ethnic groups were found. One major pattern uncovered was that the acculturation rate of Chinese American women was faster than all other Asian American groups tested.

436. Wong, Kay S. "Chinese-American Women: A Phenomenological Study of Self-Concept." Ph.D. diss., The Wright Institute, 1983.

The self-concept of five first-generation Chinese American women was studied using a phenomenological research method consisting of two open-ended, in-depth interviews with the participants to determine their sense of self. One objective of the study was to facilitate clinical treatment of these women. Findings suggest that the self-concepts of these women reflect their Chinese cultural heritage and an autonomous self-concept is a reflection of American values.

437. Yanagida, Evelyn, and Anthony J. Marsella. "The Relationship Between Depression and Self-Concept Discrepancy Among Different Generations of Japanese-American Women." *Journal of Clinical Psychology* 34 (July 1978): 654-658.

Studied the relationship between self-concept and depression across four generations of Japanese American women in Hawaii. The younger generations had higher depression symptomatology scores which suggest that the older generations of Japanese Americans in Hawaii may be experiencing an acculturative process that differs from that of the younger generations.

438. Yanagisako, Sylvia J. "Women-Centered Kin Networks in Urban Bilateral Kinship." *The American Ethnologist* 4, no.2 (May 1977): 207-226.

Analyzes female-centered kinship networks among second-generation Japanese Americans in Seattle. Says that cultural values and awareness of their vulnerability because of their minority status led Japanese Americans to emphasize solidarity among female kin.

CHAPTER 3

HISPANIC AMERICAN WOMEN

This chapter lists publications on Mexican American, Puerto Rican, and Cuban American women. Included here are English-language materials only. The bulk of the literature is concerned with Chicanas.

Much of the scholarly literature on Hispanic women focuses on their role in the family and the impact outside employment has on it. Hispanic American women have a long tradition of working outside the home and have made a positive contribution to supporting their families as many of the items in this section demonstrate.

There are a handful of comprehensive, book-length works on Mexican American women which form the core of the literature in this area. Among these are *La Chicana* by Alfredo Mirande, and *Diosa y Hembra: The History and Heritage of Chicanas in the United States* by Martha P. Cotera. In the past ten years there has been a definite upsurge in the publication of both book-length studies and journal articles on the subject of Hispanic women.

A great deal of the published material on Mexican American women is concerned with countering the negative images of Chicanas depicted in both the popular media and in social science scholarship. Several essays and articles discuss the Chicana reaction to the women's movement and the need to achieve equality with Chicanos in the Chicano movement.

Another area of current interest in which the literature is growing is discussion and analysis of the work of Chicana poets. A recent book has been published on the subject and there are a number of journal articles concerned with this topic.

Bibliographies

439. Cotera, Martha P. *Latina Sourcebook: Bibliography of Mexican American, Cuban, Puerto Rican and Other Hispanic Women Materials in the USA.* Austin, Texas: Information Systems Development, 1982.

A partially annotated bibliography covering Cuban, Mexican, and Puerto Rican heritage women in the United States. Includes reference materials, journal articles, ERIC documents, curriculum materials and other sources useful for grade school and high school students, and audiovisual materials.

440. Loeb, Catherine. "La Chicana: A Bibliographic Survey." *Frontiers* 5, no.2 (1980): 59-74.

A bibliographic essay which overviews recent English-language materials emphasizing easily accessible works. Provides a good introduction to the subject for researchers/readers.

441. Sweeney, Judith. "Chicana History: A Review of the Literature." in *Essays on La Mujer.* Edited by Rosauru Sanchez and Rosa Martinez Cruz. Los Angeles, Calif.: University of California, Los Angeles, 1977, pp. 99-123.

A bibliographical essay divided by major historical periods from 1519 to 1976. Besides historical studies, it also includes the topics of employment, social conditions, the Chicana in the family, and literature. A good overview and introduction to the subject.

442. Zinn, Maxine B. "Mexican Heritage Women: A Bibliographic Essay." *Sage Race Relations Abstracts* 9 (August 1984): 1-12.

Identifies major issues and sources of information in the social science literature concerning Mexican American women.

General Works

443. Bose, Christine E. "The Puerto Rican Woman in the United States: An Overview." in *The Puerto Rican Woman.* 2nd ed. Edited by Edna Acosta-Belan. New York: Praeger, 1986, pp. 147-169.

Presents an overall statistical portrait of Puerto Rican women in the United States covering the areas of labor force participation, income, education, family composition, marital status, and fertility rates.

444. Brinson-Pineda, Barbara. "Hispanic Women Toward an Agenda for the Future." in *Beyond Sex Roles*. 2nd ed. Edited by Alice G. Sargent. New York: West Publishing Co., 1985, pp. 252-257.

     An article which overviews some of the major issues of concern to Hispanic women such as increased access to educational and employment opportunities.

445. Cotera, Martha P. *Diosa y Hembra: The History and Heritage of Chicanas in the United States*. Austin, Texas: Information Systems Development, 1976.

     Intended to provide a broad overview or profile of Mexican American women, it was the first comprehensive treatment available on La Chicana. The first part of the book contains an historical outline from the Pre-Columbian period until 1960. The second half has sections on contemporary issues such as education, employment, the family, and Chicanas and feminism.

446. Jorge, Angela. "The Black Puerto Rican Woman in Contemporary American Society." in *The Puerto Rican Woman*. 2nd ed. Edited by Edna Acosta-Belan. New York: Praeger, 1986, pp. 180-187.

     Discusses the unique situation of the black Puerto Rican woman in the United States who is discriminated against by her own culture as well as the dominant white society.

447. King, Lourdes M. "Puertorriquenas in the United States: The Impact of Double Discrimination." *Civil Rights Digest* 6, no.3 (Spring 1974): 20-27.

     Profiles the economic and life situation of Puerto Rican women in the United States and the impact of racial and sexual discrimination upon it.

448. Melville, Margarita, ed. *Twice a Minority: Mexican American Women*. St. Louis, Mo.: C.V. Mosby, 1980.

     Contains scholarly articles on a variety of topics. Contains items 488, 492, 531, and 536.

449. Mirande, Alfredo. *La Chicana: The Mexican American Woman*. Chicago, Ill.: University of Chicago Press, 1979.

     One of the few book-length treatments on Chicanas, this is a comprehensive work on the subject. It contains chapters on the cultural heritage of Mexico and the Southwest, the role of women in the family, work and education, images in literature, and Chicana feminism. Its main thesis is that the cultural heritage of colonial Mexico and the American Southwest is of primary importance in understanding the situation of the contemporary Mexican American woman.

* See also item 305

Autobiography, Biography, Life Histories

450. Elsasser, Nan et al. *Las Mujeres: Conversations from a Hispanic Community.* Old Westbury, New York: The Feminist Press, 1980.

A collection of life stories of Hispanic women from New Mexico transcribed from taped interviews. Includes women with varying backgrounds, occupations, interests and from different age groups.

451. Gonzalez, Elizabeth Q. "The Education and Public Career of Maria L. Urquides: A Case Study of a Mexican American Community Leader." Ed.D. diss., University of Arizona, 1986.

A life history which describes and evaluates the career of Dr. Maria L. Urquides, a Mexican American woman who is a leader in education and the Hispanic community. Concludes that Dr. Urquides was able to retain her ties with her cultural background, and she exhibits strong coping skills and a positive attitude in life.

452. "Maria Elena." in *Dignity: Lower Income Women Tell of Their Lives and Struggles.* Edited by Fran Leeper Buss. Ann Arbor, Michigan: University of Michigan Press, 1985, pp. 246-281.

This is the life story of the daughter of migrant laborers. The oldest of seventeen children, she worked with her parents in the fields. As an adult she became a United Farm Workers organizer.

453. Sheehan, Susan. *A Welfare Mother.* Boston: Houghton Mifflin, 1976.

Tells the story of Carmen Santana, a Puerto Rican mother living on welfare in Brooklyn with a large family to support. Written in a journalistic style, it is concerned with exposing the failures of the welfare system. It portrays Mrs. Santana sympathetically as a victim of the system.

Education

454. Casas, J. Manuel, and Ponterotto, Joseph G. "Profiling an Invisible Minority in Higher Education: The Chicana." *Personnel and Guidance Journal* 12 (February 1984): 349-352.

Reports the results of a study of forty-six Chicana college
students attending schools in the Santa Barbara area. Concludes
that although these students do well academically, they face
barriers of inadequate academic preparation and lack of financial
resources which discourage Chicanas from completing higher
education programs in greater numbers. Recommends that colleges set up task forces to stimulate increased enrollment of
Mexican American women.

455. Chacon, Maria et al. *Chicanas in Postsecondary Education.*
      Stanford, California: Center for Research on Women, Stanford
      University, 1982.

      Describes the experiences of Chicanas attending institutions of
      higher education. Makes a number of recommendations to
      facilitate the retention of Chicanas and Chicanos in universities
      and colleges. Concludes that minority-oriented services are very
      important for those students who are from poorer, less-educated
      immigrant or first generation families. Suggests that women's
      programs should reach out to younger minority women who may
      need peer support as much as older reentry women students.
      Also recommends the need for special orientation courses for
      reentry women.

456. Esparaza, Mariana O. "The Impact of Adult Education on Mexican-
      American Women." Ed.D. diss., Texas A and I University, 1981.

      The purpose of this study was to gather data concerning the
      importance of adult education classes in meeting the career
      orientation needs, aspirations and self-perceptions of women be-
      tween the ages of seventeen and sixty. Found that the younger
      women were more career oriented, while the older women were
      more traditional. Suggests that personnel in adult education
      need to allow for age differences in helping Mexican American
      women, and says more career orientation counseling is needed.

457. Estrada, Rosa O. "A Study of the Attitudes of Texas Mexican
      American Women Toward Higher Education." Ed.D. diss., Bayler
      University, 1985.

      Examines attitudes of Texas Mexican American women toward
      higher education. Questionnaires were administered to 403
      Chicanas from seven Texas cities. Findings indicate that Latina
      women in Texas have a positive attitude toward education and
      they believe that it leads to advanced and improved status.

458. Gandara, Patricia. "Passing Through the Eye of the Needle: High-
      Achieving Chicanas." *Hispanic Journal of Behavioral Sciences* 4,
      no.2 (1982): 167-179.

Identified background factors and experiences which contributed
to the success of a group of seventeen Mexican American women
between the ages of twenty-eight and forty. They all came
from lower socio-economic backgrounds, but had succeeded in
completing J.D., M.D., and Ph.D. degrees. It was found that the
emotional support of their families and the strong role models
their mothers provided were important factors contributing to
their achievement.

459. Lopez, Gloria A. "Job Satisfaction of the Mexican American Woman
      Administrator in Higher Education." Ph.D. diss., University of
      Texas at Austin, 1984.

      Investigated the job satisfaction of Mexican American women
      administrators in higher education. Collected data from 147
      women living in seven states of the Southwest. Found that
      there has been minimal integration of Hispanic women into
      administrative positions in higher education. The participants in
      this study primarily held mid-management level positions as
      directors and coordinators. They expressed satisfaction with
      their current positions, but their expectations for future
      advancement were low.

460. Montenegro, Raquel. "Educational Implications of Cultural Values
      and Attitudes of Mexican-American Women." Ph.D. diss.,
      Claremont Graduate School, 1973.

      Surveyed young women (ages seventeen to twenty-four) of
      Mexican descent living in a low socioeconomic urban area of Los
      Angeles in order to determine their attitudes and beliefs
      concerning education and vocational choices. Results indicated
      that the participants in the study were proud of their heritage,
      but rejected the dominant role of the husband in traditional
      Mexican families. They were strongly committed to continuing
      their education.

461. Ortiz, Flora I. "The Distribution of Mexican American Women in
      School Organizations." *Hispanic Journal of Behavioral Sciences* 4,
      no.2 (1982): 181-198.

      Asserts that Mexican American women in public school
      administration are assigned, on a temporary basis, to head
      special projects or to head schools which are deemed problem
      schools. Says that because of this practice, they are pre-
      vented from advancing their careers.

462. Terrazas, Luis M. "The Psychological Effects of Adult Basic
      Education Programs on Locus of Control and Socialization in
      Mexican-Born Mexican American Women." Ph.D. diss., United
      States International University, 1977.

One hundred and fifty-nine Mexican-born Mexican American women whose native language was Spanish and who were enrolled in Adult Basic Education Programs in San Diego County, California formed the sample for this study. It was concerned with the impact this program had on locus of control and socialization of this group of participants. It was concluded that adult education had no significant influence on locus of control and socialization for the subjects.

463.   Torres, Cynthia. "Cultural and Psychological Attributes and Their Implications for Career Choice and Aspirations Among Mexican American Females." Ph.D. diss., University of California, Los Angeles, 1986.

Investigated cultural and psychological factors such as degree of biculturalism and self-esteem on the career choice and aspirations of Mexican American female high school students. The purpose of the study was to identify the counseling needs of young Mexican American female students and provide educators with a career counseling framework for these students.

464.   Vasquez, Melba J.T. "Chicana and Anglo University Women: Factors Related to Their Performance, Persistence and Attrition." Ph.D. diss., The University of Texas at Austin, 1978.

A study of factors influencing successful completion of college among female Mexican American students. Factors considered were academic background, demographic characteristics, psycho-social characteristics, and degree of bicultural identity. Results indicated that high school grade point average, socioeconomic status, and perception of importance of graduation to mother were variables which contributed to the success in college of the Mexican American students.

465.   Vasquez, Melba J.T. "Confronting Barriers to the Participation of Mexican American Women in Higher Education." *Hispanic Journal of Behavioral Sciences* 4, no.2 (1982): 147-165.

Identifies major barriers preventing Chicanas from participating in and completing programs of higher education, such as low socioeconomic status, parental inability to finance higher education, and alienation and lack of support in the college environment. Makes recommendations for removing these barriers.

Employment

466. Blair, Leita M. "Characteristics of Professional and Traditional
      Mexican American Women Related to Family Origin, Role Models,
      and Conflicts: A Case Study." Ed.D. diss., East Texas State
      University, 1984.

      Conducted interviews with eight professional and eight
      traditional Hispanic women in order to compare and describe the
      two groups. It was concluded that differences in families of
      origin and early role models may have influenced their choice of
      role.

467. Calderon, Vivian. "Maternal Employment and Career Orientation of
      Young Chicana, Black, and White Women." Ph.D. diss.,
      University of California, Santa Cruz, 1984.

      Studied the influence of maternal employment on career choices
      and work commitment for young women between the ages of
      sixteen and twenty-two. For all ethnic groups, maternal
      employment had a positive influence. Particularly noted the way
      maternal employment lessened traditional gender role attitudes
      among Chicanas.

468. Cardenas, Gilbert et al. "Undocumented Immigrant Women in the
      Houston Labor Force." *California Sociologist* 5 (Summer 1982):
      98-118.

      Reports the results of a study of undocumented female
      immigrant workers in the Houston area. Asserts that
      undocumented women workers have fared better than has been
      predicted by observers. Says that beyond the entry level long-
      term undocumented workers are at a disadvantage because of
      their illegal status.

469. Cooney, Rosemary S. "Changing Labor Force Participation of
      Mexican American Wives: A Comparison with Anglos and Blacks."
      Social Science Quarterly 56 (September 1975): 252-261.

      Analyzes and compares labor force participation rates for
      married Mexican American women with rates for Anglos and
      blacks using data from the 1960 and 1970 censuses.
      Demonstrates that Mexican American wives with either a college
      education or with pre-school children have increased their labor
      force participation rates in the decade between 1960 and 1970.
      Says that changes within the Mexican American family have
      occurred to account for this change.

470. Cooney, Rosemary S. "Intercity Variations in Puerto Rican Female Participation." *Journal of Human Resources* 14, no.2 (Spring 1979): 222-235.

   Analyzes the question of why Puerto Rican female labor force participation has declined in New York by comparing it to Chicago where it has increased. This study, based on 1970 census data, shows that labor market conditions in Chicago are more favorable thus keeping Puerto Rican women in the labor force.

471. Cooney, Rosemary S., and Alice E. Colon. "Declining Female Participation Among Puerto Rican New Yorkers: A Comparison with Native White Non-Spanish New Yorkers." *Ethnicity* 6 (September 1979): 281-297.

   Says that the Puerto Rican female labor force has declined in New York between 1960-1970 because the changing labor market requires more highly educated and skilled employees which has adversely affected less-educated Puerto Rican women.

472. Cooney, Rosemary S., and Alice E. Colon. "Work and Family: The Recent Struggles of Puerto Rican Females." in *The Puerto Rican Struggle*. Edited by Clara E. Rodriguez et al. New York: Puerto Rican Migration Research Consortium Inc., 1980, pp. 58-73.

   Says the relative economic position of Puerto Ricans has deteriorated due to the growth of female-headed households and the decline of labor force participation of Puerto Rican women. Suggests that this has happened because Puerto Rican women lack upgraded educational requirements and the skills needed to enter the new industrial structure in the New York region.

473. Cooney, Rosemary S., and Vilma Ortiz. "Nativity, National Origin, and Hispanic Female Participation in the Labor Force." *Social Science Quarterly* 64, no.3 (1983): 510-523.

   Examines differences and similarities in the correlation of education, English language proficiency, and household headship with labor force participation among native-born Hispanic women and Cuban, Mexican, and Puerto Rican women born outside the United States. The pattern of findings indicate that native-born women are integrated into the work force to a greater extent than women born outside the United States, and the availability of low-skilled jobs significantly affected the participation of foreign-born Hispanic women.

474. Coyle, Laurie et al. "Women at Farah: An Unfinished Story." in *Mexican Women in the United States: Struggles Past and*

Present. Edited by Magdalena Mora and Adelaida R. Del Castillo. Los Angeles, Calif.: Chicano Studies Research Center Publications, University of California, 1980, pp. 117-143.

An account of a strike by four thousand largely Mexican American female garment workers at Farah Manufacturing Company in El Paso, Texas in 1972-1974. This account is based on extensive interviews with the participants.

475. Enriquez-White, Celia. "Attitudes of Hispanic and Anglo Women Managers Toward Women in Management." Ed.D. diss., University of La Verne, 1982.

Compared the attitudes of one hundred Anglo female managers to one hundred Hispanic female managers in the state of California in order to investigate the way in which Latina women view women managers. Results indicated no difference between the attitudes of the two groups of women, and concluded that both have a positive attitude towards women in management.

476. Ferree, Myra M. "Employment Without Liberation: Cuban Women in the United States." *Social Science Quarterly* 60, no.1 (June 1979): 35-50.

Says that increased employment of Cuban women in the United States has not significantly changed the traditional role of women in the family.

477. Gonzalez, Rosalinda M. "Chicanas and Mexican Immigrant Families, 1920-1940." in *Decades of Discontent: The Women's Movement, 1920-1940*. Edited by Lois Scharf and Joan M.Jensen. Westport, Conn.: Greenwood Press, 1983, pp. 59-84.

Documents the labor history of Mexican immigrants and Chicanas in the Southwest during the 1920s and 1930s. Clarifies the underlying economic conditions in Mexico and the United States which contributed to the sexual, racial and class exploitation of Mexican American women.

478. Hancock, Paula F. "The Effects of Nativity, Legal Status and Welfare Eligibility on the Labor Force Participation of Women of Mexican Origin in California." Ph.D. diss., University of Southern California, 1985.

Analyzes differences in the labor force participation of native-born, legal, and undocumented women of Mexican origin. Finds that married, native-born women have higher work rates than Mexican-born women. Concludes that the undocumented women work out of extreme necessity.

*   Higginbotham, Elizabeth. "Laid Bare by the System: Work and
        Survival for Black and Hispanic Women." in *Class, Race, and
        Sex: The Dynamics of Control.* Edited by Amy Swerdlow and
        Hanna Lessinger. Boston: G.K. Hall, 1983, pp. 200-215.

        Cited above as item 117.

479.   Hurst, Marsha, and Ruth E. Zambrana. "Child Care and Working
        Mothers in Puerto Rican Families." *Annals of the American
        Academy of Political and Social Science* 461 (May 1982):
        113-124.

        Concludes that lack of adequate child care arrangements is a
        factor in the lowered employment rates of Puerto Rican women
        in the New York area. Suggests that public policy be directed
        toward restructuring the work situation so that child care can
        be provided by parents or relatives.

480.   Korrol, Virginia S. "Survival of Puerto Rican Women in New York
        before World War II." in *The Puerto Rican Struggle.* Edited by
        Clara E. Rodriguez et al. New York: Puerto Rican Migration
        Research Consortium, Inc., 1980, 47-57.

        Based on census data from the 1925 New York State Census and
        seventy-five oral interviews. Outlines ways in which Puerto
        Rican women were able to supplement family incomes through
        in-home piecework, child care, and taking in lodgers while
        avoiding sex role conflicts.

481.   Martinez, Elizabeth, and Ed McCaughan. "Chicanas and Mexicanas
        in a Transnational Working Class." in *The Future of Women.*
        Edited by Marlene Dixion. San Francisco, Calif.: Synthesis
        Publications, 1983, pp. 146-180.

        A Marxist interpretation of the role of Chicanas in the United
        States labor force. Focuses on the devaluation of
        Chicana/Mexicana domestic labor in the home and undervaluation
        of their labor in the work place.

482.   Mindiola, Tatcho. "The Cost of Being a Mexican Female Worker in
        the 1970 Houston Labor Market." *Aztlan: International Journal of
        Chicano Studies Research* 11, no.2 (Fall 1980): 231-248.

        Calculates an estimate of discrimination in employment of
        Mexican American females compared to Anglo males for the
        Houston area in 1970. Found that Mexican American women
        earned higher wages and experienced less discrimination in

government jobs. Whereas, discrimination was the most severe in service industries and sales according to this article.

483.   Ortiz, Vilma, and Rosemary S. Cooney. "Sex-Role Attitudes and Labor Force Participation Among Young Hispanic Females and Non-Hispanic White Females." *Social Science Quarterly* 65 (June 1984): 392-400.

Found that first-generation Hispanic women had more traditional sex role attitudes than did second or third-generation Hispanic American females or non-Hispanic white females, and first and second-generation Hispanic females were less likely to be employed outside the home than non-Hispanic white females. Says this difference in labor force participation is due to variations in educational attainment not to traditional sex role attitudes.

484.   Romero, Mary. "Twice Protected? Assessing the Impact of Affirmative Action on Mexican-American Women." in *Ethnicity and Women*. Edited by Winston A. Van Horne and Thomas V. Tonnesen. University of Wisconsin System, American Ethnic Studies Coordinating Committee, 1986, pp. 134-156.

Maintains that affirmative action employment policies have not benefited Mexican American females at the expense of white males as has been alleged. Says that despite affirmative action, white males maintain a larger share of higher-paying and skilled jobs in private industry.

485.   Segura, Denise. "Labor Market Stratification: The Chicana Experience." *Berkeley Journal of Sociology* 29 (1984): 57-91.

Analyzes wage differentials and discrimination in the labor market as they pertain to Chicanas. Maintains that a triple oppression of race, class and gender operates to restrain Chicanas from obtaining socioeconomic equality in society. Says this triple oppression inhibits Chicanas from acquiring the skills and credentials to compete for jobs.

486.   Simoniello, Katina. "On Investigating the Attitudes Toward Achievement and Success in Eight Professional U.S. Mexican Women." *Aztlan: International Journal of Chicano Studies Research* 12, no.1 (Spring 1981): 121-137.

The women in this study identified education, close relationship with family, identification with their mothers, and mentoring as factors influencing their success in nontraditional careers. All of the women had experienced racial and gender discrimination in attaining their professional goals.

487. Taylor, Paul S. "Mexican Women in Los Angeles Industry in 1928."
Aztlan: International Journal of Chicano Studies Research 11,
no.1 (Spring 1980): 99-131.

This article is based on field research originally conducted in
the 1920s of Mexican American women employed in factories and
canneries in Los Angeles. Interesting because of its historical
perspective.

488. Whiteford, Linda. "Mexican American Women as Innovators." in
Twice a Minority: Mexican American Women. Edited by Margarita Melville. St. Louis, Mo.: C.V. Mosby, 1980, pp. 109-126.

Researched the role of women as innovators of social change in
a small region of Texas on the United States-Mexican border.
Women who were born into families of migrant laborers were
able to better the economic situation of their families by taking
advantage of new job openings in service areas. Found that
these women had fewer children and they had a more egalitarian
role in family decisions as a result of their improved
employment status.

489. Zavella, Patricia. "The Impact of 'Sun Belt Industrialization' on
Chicanas." in *The Women's West.* Edited by Susan Armitage
and Elizabeth Jamison. Norman, Oklahoma: University of
Oklahoma Press, 1987, pp. 291-304.

Argues that Chicanas value work outside the home in contrast
to the cultural stereotype which portrays Hispanic women as
traditional housewives. Twenty-two married Chicana workers,
who had at least one child under the age of six, were
interviewed for this study. They were employed in either the
electronics or the garment industries in Albuquerque, New
Mexico. Concludes that the wages of these women are essential
to support their families, and sees this as part of the nationwide
trend toward two-paycheck families.

490. Zavella, Patricia. *Women's Work and Chicano Families: Cannery
Workers of the Santa Clara Valley.* Ithaca, New York: Cornell
University Press, 1987.

In this anthropological study of women cannery workers in San
Jose, California, Zavella is concerned with the connection
between Chicano family life and ethnic and gender inequality in
the labor market. The research method used consisted of in-
depth interviews with twenty-four women, and was originally
conducted in 1977-1978. She concludes that although women
who work part-time in canneries have more power in the family
than women who do not work, women's employment does not
lead to more egalitarian family structures as other researchers

have asserted. Family conflict and traditional patriarchal family notions were evident in the informants' family life.

491. Zinn, Maxine B. "Employment and Education of Mexican-American Women: The Interplay of Modernity and Ethnicity in Eight Families." *Harvard Educational Review* 50, no.1 (February 1980): 47-62.

Focuses on the role of Chicanas as wives and the impact of outside employment and level of education on family life and ethnicity. It was found that as women acquired additional education and work outside the family, they achieved greater equality in family decision making without giving up their ethnicity.

Feminism and Women's Studies

492. Cotera, Marta. "Feminism: The Chicana and Anglo Versions: A Historical Analysis." in *Twice a Minority: Mexican American Women*. Edited by Margarita B. Melville. St. Louis, Mo.: C.V. Mosby, 1980, pp. 217-234.

Asserts that Chicanas have been excluded from and discriminated against in both waves of the women's movement.

493. Cotera, Martha P. *The Chicana Feminist*. Austin, Texas: Information Systems Development, 1977.

Contains brief, previously published magazine articles and transcripts of speeches. There is little of substance in this collection.

494. De Valdez, Theresa A. "Organizing as a Political Tool for the Chicana." *Frontiers* 5, no.2 (1980): 7-13.

Outlines the difficulties and dilemmas faced by Mexican American women in organizing to confront racism and sexism in the dominant society. Says that Chicanas have benefited from the women's movement, but that it has limited potential as a resource for Hispanic women. Asserts that Mexican American women must work within their own culture to achieve self-determination and equality.

495. Enriquez, Evangelina, and Alfredo Mirande. "Liberation, Chicana style: Colonial Roots of Feministas Chicanas." *De Colores* 4, no.3 (1978): 7-21.

Traces the feminist tradition within Mexican and Mexican American cultures. Argues that contemporary Chicanas are triply oppressed. Says they suffer internal oppression within their own culture as well as discrimination on account of their sex and their race. Discusses Chicana discontent with both the Chicano liberation movement and the Anglo women's movement. Advocates that Chicanos and Chicanas work together as equal partners in the struggle against their mutual oppression.

496. Gonzales, Sylvia. "La Chicana: Guadalupe or Malinche." in *Comparative Perspectives on Third World Women*. Edited by Beverly Lindsay. New York: Praeger, 1980, pp. 224-250.

An analysis of the dual images of Mexican and Mexican American women as virgins and fallen women/betrayers in Mexican American culture. Says that Chicana feminism need not necessarily lead to the destruction of the family. It may lead to serious scholarship, cultural analysis, and group self-criticism according to Gonzales.

497. Gonzales, Sylvia. "Toward a Feminist Pedagogy for Chicana Self-Actualization." *Frontiers* 5, no.2 (1980): 48-51.

Advocates using feminist education as a tool for empowering Chicanas. Says that otherwise Mexican American women will continue to be underemployed and socially isolated.

498. Gonzales, Sylvia. "The White Feminist Movement: the Chicana Perspective." *Social Science Journal* 14, no.2 (April 1977): 67-76.

Decries the negative images of Chicanas in the media, literature, and social science research. Says that within the Mexican American community the accomplishments of Chicanas have been unrecognized. Asserts that there can be no real unity between Chicanas and Chicanos until the struggles of women are supported. Recommends inclusion of the Chicana perspective in women's studies courses.

499. Jorge, Angela. "Issues of Race and Class in Women's Studies: A Puerto Rican Woman's Thoughts." in *Class, Race, and Sex: The Dynamics of Control*. Edited by Amy Swerdlow and Hanna Lessinger. Boston: G.K. Hall, 1983, pp. 216-220.

Urges the need to address the issues of class and race in the women's movement with particular reference to the perspective of the Puerto Rican woman in America.

* See also item 175.

500. Votaw, Carmen D. "Cultural Influences on Hispanic Feminism." *Agenda* 11, no.4 (1981): 44-49.

Says that Hispanic females have had reservations about joining the women's movement because it has been defined by the extreme right as an effort to destroy the family. This runs counter to the Hispanic concept of the close-knit family as a buffer against adversity and a way of preserving Hispanic culture and traditions.

History and Politics

501. Apodaca, Maria L. "The Chicana Woman: An Historical Materialist Perspective." *Latin American Perspectives* 4, nos.1 and 2 (Winter and Spring 1977): 70-89.

A Marxist interpretation of the role of women in Mexican and Mexican American cultures. Says that capitalism and male chauvinism have combined to oppress Mexican American women and to prevent study of the Chicana.

502. Candelaria, Cordelia. "La Malinche, Feminist Prototype." *Frontiers* 5, no.2 (1980): 1-6.

A vindication of the role of Marina, the Indian woman who assisted Cortes in the conquest of Mexico. Argues that she adapted to the historical circumstances thrust upon her, thereby defying traditional expectations of a woman's role. Asserts that she provides a positive model for contemporary Mexican American women.

503. Garcia, Mario T. "The Chicano in American History: The Mexican Women of El Paso, 1880-1920: A Case Study." *Pacific Historical Review* 49 (May 1980): 315-337.

Uses a case study approach of the Mexican women of El Paso, Texas, in the period between 1880 and 1920 to portray the roles of Mexican American women as housewives, wage workers, and labor union activists in the United States.

504. Hernandez, Patricia. "Lives of Chicana Activists." in *Mexican Women in the United States: Struggles Past and Present*. Edited by Magdalena Mora and Adelaida R. Castillo. Los Angeles, Calif.: Chicano Studies Research Center Publications, University of California, 1980, pp. 17-25.

Interviews with two Chicana activists who began their political involvement with the Chicano Student Movement at San Diego State University in the late 1960s. Concentrates on how their activism influenced their personal lives.

505. Lecompte, Janet. "The Independent Women of Hispanic New Mexico, 1821-1846." *Western Historical Quarterly* 12 (January 1981): 17-35.

Outlines women's social and legal rights such as the right to seek divorce in the Alcalde courts of New Mexico during the Republican period. Says these rights were later curtailed in the American courts.

506. Madrigal, Rayes R. "La Chicana and the Movement: Ideology and Identity." Ph.D. diss., Claremont Graduate School, 1977.

A study of Chicana activists in the Los Angeles area. The purpose of the study was to identify conditions which contribute to increased participation in Chicano political organizations. The results of the study indicate that women of middle to upper income tend to identify more with Chicano political organizations, while Mexican American women who were religiously committed did not participate in these organizations.

507. Zinn, Maxine B. "Political Familism: Toward Sex Role Equality in Chicano Families." *Aztlan* 6 (Spring 1975): 13-26.

Asserts that involvement of Chicanas in the Chicano liberation movement has weakened traditional patriarchal patterns in Mexican American families and has functioned to equalize sex roles.

Literature

508. Cota-Cardenas, Margarita. "The Chicana in the City as Seen in Her Literature." *Frontiers* 6, no.1 (1981): 13-18.

Explores themes in the poetry of Chicanas in the city such as alienation, conflicts of attitudes between Chicanas and Chicanos, anxiety about the use of drugs, and ambivalence in conforming to the value systems of two cultures.

* Fisher, Jerilyn B. "The Minority Woman's Voice: A Cultural Study of Black and Chicano Fiction." Ph.D. diss., The American University, 1978.

Cited above as item 256.

509. Lindstrom, Naomi. "Four Representative Hispanic Women Poets of Central Texas: A Portrait of Plurality." *Third Woman* 2, no.1 (1984): 64-70.

Comments on the work of four local Hispanic women poets: Angela de Hoyor, Rosa Raqual Elizondo, Beatriz Beltran and

Carmen Tafolla. Says that their poetry allows the emergence of a portrait of cultural plurality.

510. Ordonez, Elizabeth. "The Concept of Cultural Identity in Chicana Poetry." *Third Woman* 2, no.1 (1984): 75-81.

Explores the poetry of a wide variety of Chicana writers, all of whom are seeking their own unique identities as women, Chicanos, and poets according to Ordonez.

511. Ordonez, Elizabeth. "Sexual Politics and the Theme of Sexuality in Chicana Poetry." in *Women in Hispanic Literature: Icons and Fallen Idols.* Edited by Beth Miller. Berkeley, Calif.: University of California Press, 1983, pp. 316-339.

Explores the theme of sexual oppression in contemporary poetry by a wide variety of Chicana poets. Says that Chicanas are beginning to overcome externally and self-imposed silence, and expose the contradictions of gender and race.

512. Rebolledo, Tey D. "Abuelitas: Mythology and Integration in Chicana Literature." in *Woman of Her Word: Hispanic Women Write.* Edited by Evangelina Vigil. Houston, Texas: Arte Publico Press, 1983, pp. 148-158.

Discusses the theme of grandmothers in the poetry and short stories of Chicana writers. Says grandmothers serve as a mythic mirror image in the journey to self-discovery of many Chicana writers. Grandmothers are associated with positive images of female wisdom, courage, independence, and self-reliance according to Rebolledo.

513. Rebolledo, Tey D. "The Bittersweet Nostalgia of Childhood in the Poetry of Margarita Cota-Cardenas." *Frontiers* 5, no.2 (1980): 31-35.

Examines the subjects of Chicano childhood and children in the poetry of Cota-Cardenas as it relates to the poets' expression of the past, present, and future.

514. Rebolledo, Tey D. "Game Theory in Chicana Poetry." in *Woman of Her Word: Hispanic Women Write.* Edited by Evangelina Vigil. Houston, Texas: Arte Publico Press, 1983, pp. 159-168.

Looks at the element of game playing as reflected in the poetry of Chicanas. States that these are games of strategy which are ritualized social forms. Says that Chicana poets are creating new images of women who are independent and refuse to play games in which women are victimized and manipulated.

515. Rebolledo, Tey D. "Soothing Restless Serpents: The Dreaded Creation and Other Inspirations in Chicana Poetry." *Third Woman* 2, no.1 (1984): 83-101.

     Discusses and provides examples of poetry in which Chicanas comment on the art of poetry and on the creative process which inspires their own poetry.

516. Salinas, Judy. "The Image of Women in Chicano Literature." *Revista Chicano Riquena* 4, no.4 (October 1976): 139-148.

     Says that the traditional dual image of women as either the evil temptress or the saintly Virgin Mary persists in Chicano literature. However, Salinas cites examples from contemporary works which, she says, offer a more realistic and acceptable image of Mexican American women.

517. Sanchez, Marta E. *Contemporary Chicana Poetry*. Berkeley, Calif.: University of California Press, 1985.

     Analyzes the themes, images, patterns, and forms in the work of four contemporary Chicana poets: Alma Villanueva, Lorna Dee Cervantes, Lucha Corpi, and Bernice Zamora. Sanchez is concerned with defining and clarifying the relationships between gender and cultural identity in the works of these four poets.

518. Sanchez, Marta E. "Judy Lucerno and Bernice Zamora: Two Dialectical Statements in Chicana Poetry." *De Colores* 4, no.3 (1978): 22-33.

     Says that the works of the two Chicana poets analyzed here do not belong in mutually exclusive categories. They both represent a statement of social conflict.

519. Trujillo, Marcella. "The Dilemma of the Modern Chicana Artist and Critic." *Heresies* 2, no.4 (1979): 5-10.

     Discusses the La Malinche/Virgin Mary theme in the poetry of Adeljiza Sosa Ridell, Lorenzo Calvello Schmidt, and Sylvia Gonzales.

520. Zamora, Bernice. "Archetypes in Chicana Poetry." *De Colores* 4, no.3 (1978): 43-52.

     Identifies classical archetypes in the poetry of Judy Lucero, Katarina Zamora, and Veronica Cunningham.

Social Science

521. Andrade, Sally J. "Social Science Stereotypes of the Mexican American Woman: Policy Implications for Research." *Hispanic Journal of Behavioral Science* 4, no.2 (1982): 223-244.

    Critically reviews the research literature pertaining to the role of the Chicana in the Mexican American family. Argues that Chicanas have either been systematically excluded or subjected to a distorted treatment in historical documentation and in social science research.

*   Brown, Shirley V. "Early Childbearing and Poverty: Implications for Social Services." *Adolescence* 17, no.66 (Summer 1982): 397-408.

    Cited above as item 353.

522. Cortese, Margaret. "Self-Disclosure by Mexican-American Women: The Effects of Acculturation and Language." Ph.D. diss., North Texas State University, 1979.

    Investigated the effects of level of acculturation and language of the interview on self-disclosure by Mexican American women during therapy sessions. Subjects were sixty-four adult first, second, and third-generation Mexican American women. The results of the study indicated that the language in which the therapy is conducted is a significant factor to the outcome of the therapy. Suggests that less acculturated Mexican American women would be more likely to use mental health services if they were available in Spanish.

523. Espin, OLiva M. "Cultural and Historical Influences on Sexuality in Hispanic/Latin Women: Implications for Psychotherapy." in *Pleasure and Danger: Exploring Female Sexuality.* Edited by Carole S. Vance. Boston: Routledge and Kegan Paul, 1984, pp. 149-164.

    Examines some of the factors which affect the development of sexuality in Hispanic women in the United States such as the internalization of attitudes that designate women as inferior to men and Hispanics as inferior to Anglos.

524. Hernandez, Aurea R. "A Comparative Study of Success in Mexican-American and Anglo-American College Women." Ph.D. diss., California School of Professional Psychology, 1976.

    Tested fear of success in Mexican American and Anglo male and female college students at California State University, Los Angeles. No differences were found with regard to fear of success either by sex or ethnicity.

525. Hidalgo, Hilda A., and Christensen, Elia H. "The Puerto Rican Lesbian and the Puerto Rican Community." *Journal of Homosexuality* 2, no.2 (Winter 1976/1977): 109-121.

Based on interviews with Puerto Rican lesbians living in the United States. Concludes that Puerto Rican lesbians are becoming more open about their sexual orientation although the Puerto Rican culture still makes it very difficult for gays to discuss their sexual preferences openly.

526. Jordan, B. Kathryn. "Discerning Real and Ideal Perceptions of Women in Michoacan and Montana." Ph.D. diss., University of Oregon, 1978.

Attempts to understand the changing sex roles and changing sex role perceptions of Mexican and Mexican American women in two cultures: Michoacan, Mexico and Bozeman, Montana. Surveys the opinions of males and females in both cultures.

527. Jordan, Rosan A. "The Folklore and Ethnic Identity of a Mexican-American Woman." Ph.D. diss., Indiana University, 1975.

Focuses on the folklore of a single individual, Mary S., who was born into a rural Mexican-American culture in Texas. Looks at the interrelationship in her life between the forces of acculturation, urbanization, upward-mobility and personal-accidental factors and their influence on the acquisition, maintenance or loss of folklore.

528. Jordan, Rosan A. "The Vaginal Serpent and Other Themes from Mexican-American Women's Lore." in *Women's Folklore, Women's Culture*. Edited by Rosan A. Jordan and Susan J. Kalcik. Philadelphia: University of Pennsylvania Press, 1985, pp. 26-44.

Uses folklore as a source of information for examining how Mexican American women view their culturally assigned roles and how they respond to cultural pressures. The author collected legends and stories concerning the theme of snakes and reptiles entering women's vaginas and impregnating them. Says that these tales represent the Mexican American woman's fear of sexual vulnerability and are reflective of the traditional submissive, long-suffering role of women in Mexican culture.

529. Kluessendorf, Avonelle D. "Role Conflict in Mexican-American College Women." Ph.D. diss., California School of Professional Psychology, 1985.

Explored the relationship between sex-role conflict and role orientation, locus of control, self-esteem and anxiety in 114 Mexican American and Anglo women. This study found that Chicanas experienced more sex-role conflict, had lower self-esteem, perceived less internal control, had less external/social control, and had more belief in the external/powerful others dimension of locus of control than did Anglo women.

530. Melville, Margarita B. "Mexican Women Adapt to Migration." *International Migration Review* 12, no.2 (Summer 1978): 225-235.

Reports research concerning mental stress of recently arrived documented and undocumented Mexican female migrants to Houston. Says these women experience stress caused by loneliness, isolation, and lack of social and kin support networks.

531. Melville, Margarita B. "Selective Acculturation of Female Mexican Migrants." in *Twice a Minority: Mexican American Women.* Edited by Margarita B. Melville. St. Louis, Mo.: C.V. Mosby, 1980, pp. 155-163.

Forty-seven recent migrants to the Houston area were interviewed in this study. Melville discovered that the rate of adjustment was related to education and employment. Recent arrivals who aspired to upward mobility were more willing to learn English and to Anglicize in order to secure better paying jobs.

*   Pugh, Clementine A. "Psychological Dimensions of Masculinity and Femininity and Attitudes Toward Women Among Black, Hispanic, and White Female College Students." Ed.D. diss., University of Massachusetts, 1982

Cited above as item 374.

532. Sanchez-Ayendez, Melba. "Puerto Rican Elderly Women: Shared Meanings and Informal Supportive Networks." in *All American Women Lives that Divide, Ties that Bind.* Edited by Johnetta B. Cole. New York: Free Press, 1986, pp. 172-186.

A study of older Puerto Rican women living in Boston which emphasizes family interdependence and the differing support provided elderly women by sons and daughters.

533. Stewart, Arleen. "'Las Mujeres De Aztlan': A Consultation with Elderly Mexican-American Women in a Socio-Historical Perspective." Ph.D. diss., California School of Professional Psychology, 1973.

Twenty-six elderly Mexican and Mexican American women living in the Southwest were interviewed in this study. The majority of the women had been the sole head of their households. The author maintains that this fact contradicts the stereotyped image of the submissive, dependent Mexican American woman depicted in the literature and the media.

534. Terrazas, Olga E. "The Self-Concept of Mexican-American Adolescent Females." Ph.D. diss., The Wright Institute, 1980.

Used a sample of 124 subjects, focusing on four subgroups within the general Mexican American population: rural, urban, low-income, and middle-income. Looked at the differences and similarities within the four subgroups of the sample. The author found a significant difference in the level of self-esteem between urban and rural subjects. However, because of the type of sampling technique used, no generalization was made to the Mexican American population as a whole.

535. Vallez, Andrea. "Acculturation, Social Support, Stress and Adjustment of the Mexican American College Woman (Southern California)." Ph.D. diss., University of Colorado at Boulder, 1984.

Studied psychological adjustment of Mexican American college women as it is affected by acculturation. Fifty-one female students enrolled in four colleges or universities in Southern California formed the sample. Determined that acculturation was not related to adjustment, but social support was correlated with self-esteem and depression. Social support networks for college women are encouraged.

536. Wagner, Roland M., and Diane M. Schaffer. "Social Networks and Survival Strategies." in *Twice a Minority: Mexican American Women*. Edited by Margarita B. Melville. St. Louis, Mo.: C.V. Mosby, 1980, pp. 173-190.

A mixed group of Mexican American, black, and Anglo women who were single heads of households living in a low-income area of San Jose, California were the subjects of this study. The authors found that single Mexican American women coped with their difficult circumstances through their involvement in extensive kinship networks whereby relatives assisted the women with child care and loaned them money in times of need.

537. Zinn, Maxine B. "Gender and Ethnic Identity Among Chicanos." *Frontiers* 5, no.2 (1980): 18-23.

Examines some of the issues raised by recent research
concerning the problem of how gender and ethnic identity
interact in the social identity of Mexican American women, and
points out the need for additional research on the subject.

538. Zinn, Maxine B. "Mexican-American Women in the Social Sciences."
      Signs: Journal of Women in Culture and Society 8, no.2 (Winter
      1982): 259-272.

Reviews some of the current social science literature on Mexican
American women, focusing on analytic issues. Believes there is
a need for careful and rigorous analysis when studying the
causes of the subordination of Chicanas, and that too much
emphasis has been placed on culture while other factors have
not been examined.

CHAPTER 4

NATIVE AMERICAN WOMEN

This chapter contains literature on American Indian women living in the United States. I have excluded materials on Native American women of Canada and Central and South America.

Since Rayna Green's excellent bibliography covers the subject from the earliest period until 1983, I have concentrated on recent literature published after 1975. I have made a few exceptions for items published between 1973 and 1975.

The bulk of the material on American Indian women comprises life stories, autobiographies, and biographies. Many of these discuss the transition from life on a reservation to urban living.

General studies form another large part of the literature of Native American women. Among these are the book-length studies by Carolyn Niethammer, *Daughters of the Earth*, and John and Donna Terrell, *Indian Women of the Western Morning*. A number of periodical articles have been published as well.

Some good anthropological and historical studies have been published in journals dealing with the role of women in matrilineal societies such as the Iroquois among other topics.

In general, scholarly studies concerning contemporary Native American women are lacking. This is an area where there is a need for further research.

Bibliographies

539. Green, Rayna. *Native American Women: A Contextual Bibliography.*
      Bloomington, Ind.: Indiana University Press, 1983.

      A selective, annotated bibliography listing 672 items. Includes
      books, periodical articles, audiovisual materials, and doctoral
      dissertations. Green attempts to include a wide range of
      materials both scholarly and popular. Her annotations are
      critical and concise. Written from a pro-Indian and pro-feminist
      viewpoint.

540. Green, Rayna. "Native American Women: A Review Essay." *Signs* 6
      (Winter 1980): 248-267.

      Discusses the literature of American Indian women
      chronologically from the nineteenth century to the present.
      Written from a feminist perspective, Green concludes that past
      studies of Native American women have depicted a stere-
      otypical view of them.

541. Koehler, Lyle. "Native Women of the Americas: A Bibliography."
      Frontiers 6, no.3 (1982): 73-101.

      A review essay followed by an unannotated bibliography.
      Includes the Indians of Mexico as well as of North America.
      The focus is on recent literature.

542. Medicine, Beatrice. "The Roles of Women in Native American
      Societies, A Bibliography." *Indian Historian* 8 (Summer 1975):
      50-53.

      A short unannotated bibliography which was developed out of a
      university course on Native American women. No indication of
      selection criteria is given.

General Works

543. Albers, Patricia, and Beatrice Medicine. *The Hidden Half: Studies
      of Plains Indian Women.* New York: University Press of
      America, 1983.

      The papers in this collection refute the popular image of Indian
      women as passive drudges by pointing out the artistic skills of
      Native American women and citing alternative sex roles of some
      Plains Indian women who assumed the role of warriors.

544. Albers, Patricia, and William R. James. "Illusion and Illumination:
      Visual Images of American Indian Women in the West." in *The*

Woman's West. Edited by Susan Armitage and Elizabeth Jameson. Norman, Oklahoma: University of Oklahoma Press, 1987, pp. 35-50.

Authors conclude that postcards produced for tourists portrayed images of Indian women which did not reflect the realities of the lives of Native Americans.

545. Green, Rayna. "The Pocahontas Perplex: The Image of Indian Women in Popular Culture." *Massachusetts Review* 16 (Autumn 1975): 698-714.

Discusses the dual image of Native American women as princesses/mythic symbols and as squaws and beasts of burden as illustrated in the Pocahontas story. Says such views make it impossible for Indian women to be seen as real.

546. Hungry Wolf, Beverly. *The Ways of My Grandmothers.* New York: William Morrow Co., 1980.

Contains life stories, legends, and teachings of women of the Blackfoot nation as recounted by the author's grandmother and other elderly women of the tribe. This is not an in-depth anthropological study, but an effort to preserve the traditions and teachings of Blackfoot women. An interesting collection of miscellaneous lore.

547. Jaimes, Marie A. "Towards a New Image of American Indian Women: The Renewing Power of the Feminine." *Journal of American Indian Education* 22 (October 1982): 18-32.

Says that Native American women must reclaim their power and strength by finding its source in the spiritual teachings of their traditional past. Gives examples of the significant part played by women in the religious practices of many Native American cultures.

548. Katz, Jane B., ed. *I Am the Fire of Time: The Voices of Native American Women.* New York: Dutton, 1977.

A mixed anthology including autobiography, poetry, oral history, fiction, prayer, and essays. It covers traditional tribal times to the present. The life histories are very brief. Not a particularly noteworthy effort.

549. Kidwell, Clara S. "The Power of Women in Three American Indian Societies." *Journal of Ethnic Studies* 6, no.3 (1979): 113-121.

Uses as examples the position of women in three Northeast woodland tribes (Objiwa, Winnebago, and Menominee) to illustrate the different cultural values upon which the status of Indian women was based and to refute the stereotypes of native women as squaws and princesses. Says that once women in these tribes fulfilled their obligatory roles as wives and mothers, they had a much greater degree of freedom in their activities than did men. For instance, they were able to take an active role in the political and religious life of the tribe.

550. Mathes, Valerie S. "A New Look at the Role of Women in Indian Society." *American Indian Quarterly* 2, no.2 (1975): 131-139.

Sets forth evidence countering the prevailing view that women in Native American societies were inferior to men. Says that Indian women had powers exceeding those of white women. Cites examples of Native American women as shamans and medicine women, as warriors, and chiefs.

551. Medicine, Beatrice. *The Native American Woman: A Perspective.* Las Cruces, New Mexico: Educational Resources Information Center, Clearinghouse on Rural Education and Small Schools, 1978.

Maintains the writings of anthropologists and historians reflect a male bias in that they depict Native American women as drudges and squaws. Medicine attempts to portray a more balanced view of native women in this overview based on secondary scholarship.

552. Niethammer, Carolyn. *Daughters of the Earth: The Lives and Legends of American Indian Women.* New York: Macmillan Publishing Co., Inc., 1977.

An all-encompassing study of Native American women of the United States. Chapters are arranged according to the life cycle of American Indian women from birth to old age. Illustrated with numerous photographs. Based on published anthropological field studies. In comparing the actual lives of Native American women to the stereotypes (princess, beast of burden), the author maintains that none of these images were true. She asserts that the lives of Indian women were not that different than the lives of pioneer white women except that native women had more independence.

553. Oshana, Maryann. "Native American Women in Westerns: Reality and Myth." *Frontiers* 6, no.3 (1981): 46-50.

Looks at the negative image of Indian women as passive victims in Hollywood films and cites examples of native women as political leaders, warriors, chiefs, religious leaders, and healers in order to contradict the stereotypes seen in popular culture.

* See also item 305.

554. Riley, Glenda. "Some European (Mis)Perceptions of American Indian Women." *New Mexico History Review* 59, no.3 (July 1984): 237-266.

Reviews and critiques the writings of eighteenth and nineteenth-century European explorers, travellers, and commentators whose biased views helped create the popular image of the American Indian woman as exploited and debased.

555. Smits, David D. "The 'Squaw Drudge': A Prime Index of Savagism." *Ethnohistory* 29, no.4 (1982): 281-306.

Analyzes the early American colonists' distorted view of Native American women as overworked squaws who were exploited by idle men. Says that white observers neglected to note the power and prestige of native women in the eastern woodlands who had the right to initiate divorce, control over their own bodies, influence in tribal decision-making and who participated in public activities.

556. Terrell, John U., and Donna M. Terrell. *Indian Women of the Western Morning, Their Life in Early America.* New York: Dial Press, 1974.

A popular treatment based on published anthropological studies. Organized topically with chapters on beginnings, status, duty, food, crafts, adornment, sex, life cycle, children, and health and physique. Aims to dispel the popular notion that Native American women were mere beasts of burden. Asserts that the patriarchal concept of male supremacy was not present in Native American cultures. Says males and females were mutually dependent on each other for survival.

557. Weist, Katherine M. "Plains Indian Women: An Assessment." in *Anthropology on the Great Plains: The State of the Art.* Edited by W. Raymond Wood and Margot Liberty. Lincoln, Nebraska: University of Nebraska Press, 1980, pp. 255-271.

An overview article of the role of women in traditional Plains Indian cultures based on published anthropological studies. Weist maintains that the ethnographic data support the view that women in Plains Indian societies had a subordinate role within the domestic sphere. However, she says that they had the option to strive for male goals, and role flexibility was an important characteristic of Plains Indian societies.

558. Wittstock, Laura W. "Native American Women: Twilight of a Long
      Maidenhood." in *Comparative Perspectives of Third World Women*.
      Edited by Beverly Lindsay. New York: Praeger, 1980, pp. 207-227.

      Addresses a number of issues of concern to contemporary Native
      American women such as lack of adequate education, forced
      sterilization, alcoholism and chemical dependency, loss of unique
      culture and language, and reaction to the feminist movement.

Autobiography, Biography, Life Histories

559. Agonito, Rosemary, and Joseph Agonito. "Resurrecting History's
      Forgotten Women: A Case Study From the Cheyenne Indians."
      Frontiers 6, no.3 (1982): 8-15.

      Pieces together a biographical sketch of a forgotten Northern
      Cheyenne woman, Buffalo Calf Road, who rescued her brother at
      the Battle on the Rosebud River and fought against Custer at
      the Battle of the Little Bighorn. Argues that this unknown
      woman and the women around her challenge the negative images
      of Plains Indian women.

560. Anderson, Owanah. *Ohoyo One Thousand: A Resource Guide of
      American Indian/Alaska Native Women, 1982*. Wichita Falls,
      Texas: Ohoyo Resource Center, 1982.

      Contains a brief listing of the accomplishments of 1,004
      American Indian and Alaskan native women.

561. Ashley, Yvonne. "'That's the Way We Were Raised:'An Oral
      Interview with Ada Damon." *Frontiers* 2, no.2 (Summer 1977):
      59-62.

      Ada Damon, who was born in 1900 on the Navajo Reservation
      near Shiprock, New Mexico, discusses her early life on the land
      and the transition to life in an Indian boarding school.

562. Bataille, Gretchen M. *American Indian Women Telling Their Lives*.
      Lincoln, Nebraska: University of Nebraska Press, 1984.

      A diverse collection of life histories and autobiographies of
      Native American women collected by anthropologists in the
      nineteenth and twentieth centuries. The purpose of the book is
      to dispel the popular image of Indian women as occupying a low
      status. The authors believe that the biases of male
      anthropologists and other observers led them to overlook the
      power that Indian women held in their societies.

563. Brand, Johanna. *The Life and Death of Anna Mae Aquash*.
      Toronto, Canada: James Lorimer, 1978.

The story of a contemporary Native American woman who was an activist in the American Indian Movement. A Micmac from Nova Scotia, Aquash was close friends with AIM leaders, Dennis Banks and Leonard Peltier. She had taken part in the occupation of Wounded Knee in 1973. She had been a fugitive from the FBI since November 1975, when her body was discovered in February, 1976 on the Pine Ridge Reservation. Written in a journalistic, investigative style, it attempts to unravel the mystery of Anna Mae's death.

564.   Canfield, Gae W. *Sarah Winnemucca of the Northern Paiutes*. Norman, Oklahoma: University of Oklahoma, 1983.

A carefully researched historical study based on archival material, newspaper accounts, and Sarah's autobiography, *Life Among the Paiutes*. Reared and educated among whites as well as her own people, throughout her life Sarah experienced conflict in trying to live in both cultures. This forms the major theme in Canfield's study. It describes Sarah's career as a scout and interpreter for the army, a mediator between the whites and the Paiutes, and as a spokesperson for the rights of Native Americans.

565.   Clark, Ella E., and Margot Edmonds. *Sacagawea of the Lewis and Clark Expedition*. Berkeley, California: University of California Press, 1980.

The primary concern of this historical account is to dispel the myths surrounding Sacagawea's life and to portray a factual account of her participation in the Lewis and Clark Expedition. Asserts that she was not the principal guide of the expedition, although it maintains that she was important as an interpreter with the Shoshones and in other ways. The most interesting part of the book is the second half which deals with Sacagawea's life after the expedition which has been little studied. Says that she was highly respected among the Shoshones, took part in tribal affairs, and was present at the signing of an important treaty.

566.   Fowler, Catherine S. "Sarah Winnemucca Northern Paiute, 1844-1891." in *American Indian Intellectuals*. Edited by Margot Liberty. St. Paul, Minnesota: West Publishing Co., 1978, pp. 33-42.

Examines the life and career of Sarah Winnemucca as a spokesperson for the rights of the Paiutes as well as other Native Americans. This is an historical study based on primary resources including Sarah's published autobiography. Fowler believes that Sarah's contributions as a leader and scholar are sometimes overlooked because of her view that Indians could succeed in adjusting to white culture given an opportunity to do so.

567. Highwalking, Belle. *Belle Highwalking: The Narrative of a Northern Cheyenne Woman.* Edited by Katherine M. Weist. Billings, Montana: Montana Council for Indian Education, 1979.

This narrative of a seventy-nine year old woman is unusual in that it tells of the life of an ordinary Native American woman who was not an artist, leader, or educator. The language of the narrative has been kept as close as possible to Highwalking's speaking voice. It describes the life and customs of the Cheyenne living on the reservation in the early twentieth century, and the changes Highwalking observed during her life.

568. "Irene Mack Pyawasit." in *Dignity: Lower Income Women Tell of Their Lives and Struggles.* Edited by Fran Leeper Buss. Ann Arbor, Michigan: University of Michigan Press, 1985, pp. 148-168.

Life story of a Native American woman of the Menominee tribe. She was born on a reservation, but was sent to a church boarding school at an early age which she describes as a negative experience. She is now an activist for Native American causes and is especially interested in recruiting Native American students to attend universities.

569. Jake, Lucille et al. "The Southern Paiute Woman in a Changing Society." *Frontiers* 7, no.1 (1983): 44-49.

Oral interviews with two elderly Southern Paiute women, Mable Drye and Marie Lehi.

570. Kelley, Jane H. *Yaqui Women: Contemporary Life Histories.* Lincoln, Nebraska: University of Nebraska Press, 1978.

An anthropological study using life history data collected from individuals living in Yaqui communities in or near Tucson, Arizona, Hermosillo, Mexico, and several Yaqui villages in Sonora, Mexico. Four life stories were selected for publication here. Although Kelley tried to obtain a cross-section of different age groups, the four narratives presented here are of older women. Offers an alternative view to most studies of the Yaqui culture which are male-centered.

571. Marriott, Alice, and Carol Rachlin. *Dance Around the Sun: The Life of Mary Little Bear Inkanish.* New York: Thomas Y. Crowell, 1977.

The memories of a Southern Cheyenne woman as written by anthropologists Marriott and Rachlin. Mary Little Bear was born in 1877 of a white father and a Cheyenne mother. She grew up on the reservation at Darlington, Oklahoma raised according to Cheyenne custom. In her later years she was active in maintaining the traditional arts and crafts of beadwork and moccasin-making which she had learned from her mother.

572. Mossiker, Frances. *Pocahontas: The Life and the Legend.* New York: Alfred E. Knopf, 1976.

Attempts to provide an accurate account of the founding of the Jamestown Colony and of the Powhatans and their culture. Offers a realistic portrayal of the life of Pocahontas.

573. Murray, Janette K. "Ella Deloria: A Biographical Sketch and Literary Analysis." Ph.D. diss., University of North Dakota, 1974.

Presents a description of Ella Deloria's family background, education, and career. A Dakota Sioux born on the Yankton Reservation in 1888, She was a teacher, speaker, author and researcher. This study is based on interviews with her friends and relatives. She worked under Franz Boas recording and translating statements by native speakers of her tribe. She served as a consultant for students and professors of anthropology at Columbia University. She collected and translated Dakota legends and stories which she published, and she worked on a dictionary of the Dakota language.

574. Nunez, Bonita W.W.C. *Spirit Woman: The Diaries and Paintings of Bonita Wa Wa Calachaw Nunez.* Edited by Stan Steiner. New York: Harper and Row, 1980.

The memoirs of a Native American woman from a Southern California tribe who was adopted at birth in 1888 by a wealthy white woman. She lived her entire life in New York City. An artist and writer, she was also active on behalf of the rights of Native Americans in the early part of this century. Her later years were lived in almost total obscurity. An unusual work.

575. Pandey, Triloki N. "Flora Zuni-A Portrait." in *American Indian Intellectuals.* Edited by Margot Liberty. St. Paul, Minnesota: West Publishing Co., 1978, pp. 217-225.

A life history based on the author's informal conversations with Flora Zuni, a member of the Zuni tribe. She is a very successful maker and seller of turquoise jewelry and has been able to improve the financial situation of her children and grandchildren.

576. Plummer, Stephen, and Suzanne Julin. "Lucy Swan Sioux Woman:
      An Oral History." *Frontiers* 6, no.3 (1982): 29-32.

      A brief interview with a seventy-one year old full-blooded Sioux
      woman who was born on the Rosebud Reservation in 1900.

577. Shaw, Anna M. *A Pima Past*. Tucson, Arizona: University of
      Arizona Press, 1974.

      An autobiography written in the form of a family saga beginning
      with her father's birth in aboriginal times. Mrs. Shaw was born
      on the Gila River Reservation near Phoenix, Arizona in 1898.
      This narrative describes the transition in her lifetime from the
      traditional way of life of her ancestors to urban life. She tells
      of her father's conversion to the Presbyterian Religion and his
      acceptance of many of the ways of white people. In her later
      years Mrs. Shaw returned to the reservation to live and was
      active in preserving and recording Pima customs and legends.

578. Stewart, Irene. *A Voice in Her Tribe: A Navajo Woman's Own
      Story*. Edited by Doris O. Dawdy and Mary Shepardson.
      Socorro, New Mexico: Ballena Press, 1980.

      The autobiography of a contemporary Native American woman, a
      Navajo community and tribal political leader.

579. Tanner, Helen H. "Coocoochee, Mohawk Medicine Woman."
      American Indian Culture and Research Journal 3, no.3 (1979):
      23-42.

      Traces the life of a Mohawk woman who lived among the
      Shawnee in Ohio during the eighteenth century. The facts of
      her life were gleaned from the narrative of a captive white boy
      who lived in her home during 1772-1773. Says she was highly
      respected by her community for her skill in preparing medicine
      and as a soothsayer.

Education and Employment

580. Baker, Nancy R. "American Indian Women in an Urban Setting."
      Ph.D. diss., Ohio State University, 1982.

      Examined the educational, marital and family backgrounds,
      employment history, and current activities of fifty Native
      American women from thirteen states, representing eighteen
      tribes. Found that compared to non-Indian urban women, the
      Native American women were less well-educated, earned less
      pay, and held lower status jobs. They also had poorer health
      and more children. However, most preferred to remain in an

urban setting where they had more comforts and advantages than on a reservation.

581. Englander, Marilyn J. "Through Their Words: Tradition and the Urban Indian Woman's Experience." Ph.D. diss., University of California, Santa Barbara, 1985.

Compares the experiences of older and younger Native American women living in the Santa Barbara and San Francisco areas. Oral histories were collected from women living in these urban areas in order to study the transition from reservation life to urban life experienced by the older generation.

582. Ferguson, Helena J.S. "A Study of the Characteristics of American Indian Professional Women in Oklahoma." Ph.D. diss., Ohio State University, 1985.

The purpose of this study was to identify the characteristics of Native American women professionals. The sample consisted of 137 women who were at least one-quarter Indian, of these, seventy questionnaires were returned. Data indicated that the majority of the women were employed in education, with business being the second major career field. The federal government was the primary employer. Continuing education was reported to be very important for professional growth, and upbringing, positive self-esteem and education were reported as being important for continued achievement.

583. Hanson, Wynne. "The Urban Indian Woman and Her Family." *Social Casework* 61, no.8 (October 1980): 476-483.

Case histories of five contemporary American Indian women who have successfully made the transition from reservation life to urban life without losing their identities as Native Americans. All of the women described here have been successful in their careers, but have experienced some role conflict in coping with their dual roles as homemakers and breadwinners.

584. Haupt, Carol M. "The Image of the American Indian Female in the Biographical Literature and Social Studies Textbooks of the Elementary Schools." Ed.D. diss., Rutgers University, 1984.

Examined twelve elementary school textbooks published during the years 1972 to 1982 in order to determine how the American Indian woman is currently portrayed. Results of the study indicated that the majority of Native American females have been depicted as active individuals and they have been portrayed accurately and objectively. Also concludes that the "Indian Princess" and "White Man's Helper" images have nearly disappeared in recently published biographies aimed at school children.

585.   Kidwell, Clara S. "The Status of American Indian Women in Higher Education." in *Conference on the Educational and Occupational Needs of American Indian Women*. United States. Department of Education. National Institute of Education. Washington, D.C.: Government Printing Office, 1980, pp. 83-121.

Reports the results of a research study in which a random sample of American Indian female students enrolled in colleges and universities were surveyed to collect their opinions as to their status in higher education. Results indicate that Native American women do not have significantly different or greater problems in obtaining an education than do male Native American students. However, it concludes that the number of Native Americans of both sexes who attend institutions of higher education is very low.

586.   Livingston, Katherine S. "Contemporary Iroquois Women and Work: A Study of Consciousness of Inequality." Ph.D. diss., Cornell University, 1974.

A study of the contemporary role of Iroquois women in the family, economy and polity. The author was interested in the participants' consciousness of power or powerlessness, equality or inequality. Concludes that they were conscious of inequality in white society but not in the reservation community.

587.   Medicine, Beatrice. "The Interaction of Culture and Sex Roles in the Schools." *Integrated Education* 19, no.1-2 (January-April 1981): 28-37.

Uses data from life histories and ethnographic studies to examine how the sex roles of Lakota Sioux women changed with the advent of reservation life. Specifically looks at the interaction and impact of boarding school education upon traditional female sex roles learned from parents.

588.   Metcalf, Ann. "From Schoolgirl to Mother: the Effects of Education on Navajo Women." *Social Problems* 23, no.5 (1976): 535-544.

Reports the results of a research study of the experiences of twenty-three Native American women who attended Indian boarding schools and its impact on adult self-esteem and maternal attitudes. It was found that those women who attended federally operated or missionary operated boarding schools experienced lower self-esteem, and it negatively influenced their role as mothers.

589. Metcalf, Ann. "Navajo Women in the City: Lessons from a Quarter-Century of Relocation." *American Indian Quarterly* 6, no.1-2 (Spring/Summer 1982): 71-89.

Outlines the impact of urbanization on Navajo women and their families based on interviews with twenty-three Navajo women living in the San Francisco Bay Area. Concludes that on the whole, the families interviewed had made a successful adjustment to urban living and they felt there were greater opportunities for jobs and economic security.

590. Scheirbeck, Helen M. "Current Educational Status of American Indian Girls." in *Conference on the Educational and Occupational Needs of American Indian Women.* United States. Department of Education. National Institute of Education. Washington D.C.: Government Printing Office, 1980, pp. 63-81.

Reports statistics on educational levels attained of Native American females. Points out the need for better statistic-keeping on all American Indians by age, sex, levels of schooling, and whether living on reservations or in urban settings.

591. Shepardson, Mary. "The Status of Navajo Women." *American Indian Quarterly* 6, no.1-2 (1982): 149-169.

Says increased educational and employment opportunities have contributed to the improved economic position and higher status of contemporary Navajo women.

592. Szasz, Margaret C. "'Poor Richard' Meets the Native American: Schooling for Young Indian Women in Eighteenth-Century Connecticut." *Pacific Historical Review* 49, no.2 (1980): 215-235.

Describes efforts to provide an education for Native American females by a Congregationalist minister in colonial Connecticut. Says their schooling only compounded the Indian students' dilemma and left them ill prepared to live in colonial society.

593. Witt, Shirley H. "Native Women in the World of Work." in *Native American Women and Equal Opportunity in the Federal Government.* United States. Department of Labor. Women's Bureau. Washington, D.C.: Government Printing Office, 1979, pp. 8-15.

Says that native women are the lowest paid and have the highest unemployment rates of any segment of the national work force.

History and Anthropology

594.   Allen, Paula G. "Beloved Woman: The Lesbians in American Indian
Cultures." *Conditions* 3, no.1 (Spring 1981): 67-87.

Surmises that lesbianism and homosexuality were probably
commonplace among aboriginal American Indians, but says that
the concept was dissimilar to the contemporary meaning of these
terms.

595.   Axtell, James. *The Indian Peoples of Eastern America: A
Documentary History of the Sexes.* New York: Oxford
University Press, 1981.

A collection of excerpts from primary sources such as life
stories of Native Americans, captivity narratives, and reports of
missionaries. Organized topically under headings such as birth,
coming of age, love and marriage and so forth. Contains a
number of documents pertaining to women.

596.   Bernstein, Alison. "A Mixed Record: The Political Enfranchisement
of American Indian Women During the Indian New Deal."
Journal of the West 23, no.3 (July 1984): 13-20.

Says that in general the political enfranchisement of American
Indian women in the 1930s encouraged them to follow the
example of their white counterparts and take part in civic and
political organizations, both tribal and state, and find work off
the reservation. However, asserts that, like white women, this
did not necessarily make their lives any more powerful.

597.   Blackwood, Evelyn. "Sexuality and Gender in Certain Native
American Tribes: The Case of Cross-Gender Females." *Signs:
Journal of Women in Society and Culture* 10, no.1 (Autumn
1984): 27-42.

Says that evidence from thirty-three Native American tribes
supports the conclusion that the cross-gender role for women
was as viable an institution as was the berdache for males.

598.   Buckley, Thomas. "Menstruation and the Power of Yurok Women:
Methods in Cultural Reconstruction." *American Ethnologist* 9,
no.1 (1982): 47-60.

Concludes that male anthropologists were indifferent to the
feminine perspective of the aboriginal Yurok culture of Northern
California which led investigators such as Kroeber to neglect or
discount valuable native testimony by female informants.
Contends that women of the aboriginal Yurok menstruated in

synchrony and made use of their shared times of seclusion for the practice of spiritual disciplines.

599. Camerino, Vicki. "The Delaware Indians as Women: An Alternative Approach." *American Indian Journal* 4, no.4 (April 1978): 2-11.

Refutes the view of missionaries and ethnographers who believed that the Delaware Indians were forced to accept an inferior position when they joined the Iroquois Confederacy and assumed the position of "women." Camerino demonstrates that Iroquois women occupied powerful and respected positions and were not necessarily considered inferior to men as white male ethnographers mistakenly supposed.

600. Clark, Laverne H. "The Girl's Puberty Ceremony of the San Carlos Apaches." *Journal of Popular Culture* 10 (Fall 1976): 431-448.

A description of the female puberty rites of the San Carlos Apaches by a folklorist and photographer.

601. Devens, Carol A. "Separate Confrontations: Indian Women and Christian Missions, 1630-1900." Ph.D. diss., Rutgers University, 1986.

Examines the role of gender in the response of women of the Ojibwa and Cree tribes to the colonization efforts of French Jesuits, British Wesleyan Methodists, and American Presbyterian missionaries from the colonial period to the nineteenth century. Says there was a striking difference between the responses of men and women. Women tried to preserve their traditional status which stressed autonomy and authority.

602. Ewers, John C. "Climate, Acculturation, and Costume: A History of Women's Clothing Among the Indians of the Southern Plains." *Plains Anthropologist* 25, no.7 (1980): 63-82.

A detailed, well-written and well-documented study of the clothing worn by Native American women of the southern plains.

603. Frisbie, Charlotte J. "Traditional Navajo Women: Ethnographic and Life History Portrayals." *American Indian Quarterly* 6, no.1-2 (Spring/Summer 1982): 11-27.

Describes the role of traditional Navajo women based on material from ten ethnographies and fourteen published life histories of Navajo men and women.

604. Grumet, Robert S. "Sunksquaws, Shamans, and Tradeswomen: Middle Atlantic Coastal Algonkian Women During the Seventeenth and Eighteenth Centuries." in *Women and*

Colonization: Anthropological Perspectives. Edited by Mona
Etienne and Eleanor Leacock. New York: Praeger, 1980, pp.
43-62.

Argues that women held leadership positions among the
Algonkian tribes of the Atlantic Coast during the period of
white colonization.

605. Jensen, Joan. "Native American Women and Agriculture: A Seneca
      Case Study." *Sex Roles* 3, no.5 (1977): 423-442.

      Says that Seneca women dominated agricultural production in the
      eighteenth century from which they derived high status and
      public power. Describes the gradual erosion of the traditional
      role and status of Seneca women through efforts of missionaries,
      the government, and reformers to withdraw women from
      agricultural production and establish male ownership of private
      property.

606. Nelson, Ann. "Women in Groups: Women's Ritual Sodalities in
      Native North America." *Western Canadian Journal of
      Anthropology* 6, no.3 (1976): 29-67.

      Analyzes ethnographic data from six American Indian tribes in
      order to correlate factors contributing to female solidarity.
      Concludes that in Native American horticultural societies such as
      the Iroquois where women inherited the major economic
      resources, and held ritual and political power, women had a high
      level of collective autonomy.

607. Perry, Richard J. "Variations on the Female Referent in
      Athabaskan Cultures." *Journal of Anthropological Research* 33
      (1977): 95-119.

      A comparative study of the concern with femaleness in two
      Athabaskan societies, the Western Apache and the Northern
      Athabaskan groups. Says that the threatening aspects of
      femaleness have been deemphasized among the Apaches of the
      Southwest and the positive connotations have gone from low in
      the North to high in the Southwest. Also the social status of
      women is higher among the Apache. Believes this change
      occurred because of the different environment of the Southwest
      in which the contribution of women as plant gatherers was
      emphasized.

608. Powers, Marla N. "Menstruation and Reproduction: An Oglala
      Case." *Signs: Journal of Women in Society and Culture* 6, no.1
      (Autumn 1980): 54-65.

Argues that myths and rituals related to female puberty in the Oglala culture and menstruation are aspects of the same phenomenon. Asserts that there is no evidence to support the view of some anthropologists who considered menstruation a symbol of defilement.

609. Powers, Marla N. *Oglala Women*. Chicago, Ill.: University of Chicago Press, 1986.

A study of the life cycle from birth to death of Lakota women based on life histories of women ranging in age from sixteen to ninety-six. Powers was interested in the degree to which traditional culture influences modern tribal life and how contemporary female behavior may be modeled after the traditional roles of women. In the first part of the book Powers examines the traditional female role as seen in the Oglala creation myths and through remembrances of pre-reservation life. The second half deals with the situation of the contemporary Oglala woman.

610. Rothenberg, Diane. "The Mothers of the Nation: Seneca Resistance to Quaker Intervention." in *Women and Colonization: Anthropological Perspectives*. Edited by Mona Etienne and Eleanor Leacock. New York: Praeger, 1980, pp. 63-87.

Contends that Seneca women's conservatism was used as a strategy to maintain their traditional control of the subsistence economy against changes imposed by Quaker missionaries.

611. Sauceda, Judith B. "From the Inner Circle: The Relationship of the Space Occupied, Past and Present, By the Southwest American Indian Woman to the Southwest Indo-Hispano Woman of Yester-year and Today." Ph.D. diss., University of Colorado, Boulder, 1979.

Investigated the relationship of the ecological space occupied by two groups of women in New Mexico: American Indian women and Indo-Hispano women. Looked at the lessons learned by Native American women on the North American continent, and subsequently adopted by the Indo-Hispano woman. The study also confirmed that the Spanish Conquest culture has influenced the culture of American Indian women.

612. Smith, Sherry L. "Beyond Princess and Squaw Army Officers' Perceptions of Indian Women." in *The Women's West*. Edited by Susan Armitage and Elizabeth Jameson. Norman, Oklahoma: University of Oklahoma Press, 1987, pp. 63-75.

A study of the observations of army officers serving on the frontier concerning their views of Native American women. The author believes Indian women served as a humanizing influence on the behavior of army officers.

613. Trigger, Bruce G. "Iroquoian Matriliny." *Pennsylvania Archaeologist* 48 (1978): 55-65.

Says that the Iroquois developed matrilocal and matrilineal societies because of the prolonged absence of men who were away much of the year hunting, fishing, fur trading, or fighting. Sees no evidence to justify the view that because women were responsible for planting crops, they, therefore, controlled the economic organizations of their societies.

614. Wilson, Terry P. "Osage Indian Women During a Century of Change, 1870-1980." *Prologue: The Journal of the National Archives* 14 (Winter 1982): 185-201.

Discusses marriage customs, schooling, and participation in tribal politics of Osage Indian women after the removal to Oklahoma.

615. Wright, Mary. "Economic Development and Native American Women in the Early Nineteenth Century." *American Quarterly* 33 (Winter 1981): 525-536.

Says that Native American women of the Pacific Northwest coast insured the success of the fur trade by acting as liaisons between the Indian and the white cultures, serving as intermediary traders, food gathers, and craft manufacturers, and as customers, employees, and service personnel.

616. Young, Mary E. "Women, Civilization, and the Indian Question." in *Clio was a Woman: Studies in the History of American Women.* Edited by Chester W. Gregory et al. Washington D.C.: Howard University Press, 1980, pp. 98-110.

Discusses the role of women among the Cherokees and the impact of white colonization. Says the role of women in Cherokee culture changed after they were converted to Christianity. Women were deprived of the ownership of land and were disenfranchised.

Literature and the Arts

617. Allen, Paula G. "'The Grace that Remains': American Indian Women's Literature." *Book Forum* 5, no.3 (1981): 376-382.

A brief discussion of such themes as loneliness and loss, racism, urban life, and anger in the work of contemporary American Indian women poets.

618. Allen, Paula G. *The Sacred Hoop*. Boston: Beacon Press, 1986.

Essays on American Indian literature and culture focusing on the woman-centered tradition in Native American societies. The first group of essays talk about the gynocentric orientation and female gods in some Native American tribes. The second section discusses oral tradition and its influence on contemporary American Indian literature. The works of Mourning Dove, Leslie M. Silko and Paula G. Allen are analyzed. The last part contains essays discussing the concerns of contemporary Native American women such as lesbianism and the development of feminism in the United States.

619. Bannan, Helen M. "Spider Woman's Web: Mothers and Daughters in Southwestern Native American Literature." in *The Lost Tradition: Mothers and Daughters in Literature*. Edited by Cathy Davidson and E.M. Broner. New York: Frederick Ungar, 1980, pp. 268-279.

This essay traces the mother-daughter relationship as reflected in the oral and written literature of the traditionally matrilineal Native American societies of the American Southwest.

620. Blicksilver, Edith. "Traditionalism vs. Modernnity: Leslie Silko on American Indian Women." *Southwest Review* 64 (Spring 1979): 149-160.

Says the major theme in the poetry and fiction of Leslie Silko is the conflict between traditionalism and modernity experienced by American Indian women in their roles as child, lover, wife, and mother. Also comments on Silko's use of traditional Pueblo folklore and nature in her writing.

621. Crow, Stephen M. "The Works of Leslie Marmon Silko and Teaching Contemporary Native American Literature." D.A. diss., University of Michigan, 1986.

Contains a biographical sketch of Silko's life and three chapters of interpretation of the content of *Laguna Woman*, *Ceremony* and *Story-teller*. Says that modern Indian literature has roots in traditional culture as well as contemporary reality.

622. Dearborn, Mary V. "A Case Study of American Indian Female Authorship." Chap. 1. in *Pochantas's Daughters: Gender and Ethnicity in American Culture*. New York: Oxford University Press, 1986, pp. 12-30.

Discusses the works of American Indian novelists, Mourning Dove and Leslie Marmon Silko, in the context of a larger study on gender and ethnicity in American literature.

623. Elliott, Karen S. "The Portrayal of the American Indian Woman in a Select Group of American Novels." Ph.D. diss., University of Minnesota, 1979.

Focuses on the portrayal of American Indian women in the works of five writers covering the period 1822 to the present. Although some of the writers studied attempt favorable portrayals, none of them allow the Indian to be human according to Elliott. She considers this to be just as detrimental as the portrayal of Indians as savages.

624. Fisher, Alice P. "The Transportation of Tradition: A Study of Zitkala-Sa and Mourning Dove, Two Transitional American Indian Writers." Ph.D. diss., City University of New York, 1979.

Examines the lives and works of two early American Indian women writers who tried to make the transition from oral to written form and bridge the gap between tradition and assimilation. Fisher says they became literary counterparts of the oral storytellers of their tribes.

625. Fisher, Dexter. "Zitkala-Sa: The Evolution of a Writer." *American Indian Quarterly* 5, no.3 (August 1979): 229-238.

Traces the life and career of Gertrude Simmons Bonnin (1876-1938) who was born of a Sioux mother and a white father. She was a writer and activist in the Pan-Indian movement of the 1920s and 1930s. Calling herself Zitkala-Sa, as a young woman she published autobiographical essays, short stories, and a collection of Indian legends.

626. Jahner, Elaine. "The Novel and Oral Tradition: An Interview with Leslie Marmon Silko." *Book Forum* 5, no.3 (1981): 383-399.

A brief interview which discusses themes in Silko's work, her current projects, and reactions of non-Indian critics to her work among other topics.

627. Jaskoski, Helen. "'My Heart Will Go Out': Healing Songs of Native American Women." *International Journal of Women's Studies* 4 (March-April 1981): 118-134.

The premise of this article is that poetry as used in the healing songs of American Indian women functioned as a healing agent. The author provides examples of lyrics and life stories of female healers from a cross-section of North American tribal groups. Some explication of the lyrics is also provided.

628. Jenkins, William W. "Three centuries of the Pocahontas Story in Literature: 1608-1908." Ph.D. diss., University of Tennessee, 1977.

Looks at the available facts concerning the Pocahontas and John Smith story, and examines the story as represented in drama, poetry, and fiction as a subject in American literature.

629. McCane-O'Connor, Mallory. "The Squaw as Artist: A Reevaluation." *Southern Quarterly* 17, no.2 (Winter 1979): 8-15.

Says that American Indian women made a tremendous contribution to the material culture of Native Americans, but they have been consistently omitted from the literature and portrayed as second-class citizens.

630. Mansfield-Kelley, Deane. "Oliver La Farge and the Indian Woman in American Literature." Ph.D. diss., University of Texas at Austin, 1979.

Discusses the portrayal of American Indian women characters in American literature from their first appearance in captivity narratives and Pocahontas plays through their present depiction in contemporary Western fiction. Emphasizes the important role of Oliver La Farge in establishing the Native American woman as a realistic character in his short stories and novels.

631. Peterson, Susan. *The Living Tradition of Maria Martinez*. New York: Kodansha International, 1977.

A large book of photographs of the work of Maria Martinez, the well-known potter from San Ilde-fonso Pueblo, New Mexico.

632. Peterson, Susan. *Maria Martinez: Five Generations of Potters*. Washington, D.C.: Renwick Galleries, 1978.

An exhibition catalog of the works of Maria Martinez.

633. Rubinstein, Charlotte S. "Native Americans: The First American Women Artists." Chap.1. in *Women Artists: From the Indian to the Present*. Boston: G.K. Hall, 1982, pp. 1-19.

Covers the traditional domestic arts of weaving, leather painting, quillwork and beading, basket making, ceramics, and architecture, as well as, twentieth-century painting and sculpture. Includes numerous illustrations and brief biographical sketches of the major artists.

634. Scarberry, Susan J. "Land Into Flesh: Images of Intimacy." *Frontiers* 6, no.3 (1982): 24-28.

Looks at the work of a cross-section of Native American women poets who incorporate in their poetry a vision of the connection between land and human life.

635.   Spivey, Richard L. *Maria*. Flagstaff, Arizona: Norland Press, 1979.

       Photographs of the life and work of the Pueblo Indian potter,
       Maria Martinez. Intended as a commentary on her art rather
       than a biographical work according to the author.

636.   Sutherland, Janet L. "Aufgehobene Welten: Orality and World View
       in the Fictional Works of N. Scott Momaday, Leslie Marmon
       Silko, and James Welch." Ph.D. diss., University of Oregon,
       1984.

       Examines the works of three major contemporary Native
       American authors individually and comparatively for evidence of
       intellectual structural organization and specific tribal and
       Western cultural world views. Says that Silko is successful at
       integrating other cultural traditions with that of her own
       culture, the Laguna Pueblo, into an artistically compelling
       pattern.

AUTHOR INDEX

Note: In the case of titles with two or more authors or editors, only the first author or editor is listed in this index.

SUBJECT INDEX